THE COMPREHENSIVE OWNERS HANDBOOK TO MALTESE

Mastering The Art Of Owning, Training, and Raising a Joyful and Well-Behaved Dog

Derrick Lucas

COPYRIGHT

DISCLAIMER

The author and publisher have made every effort to ensure the accuracy and completeness of the information contained in this book. However, they assume no responsibility for errors, inaccuracies, omissions, or any other inconsistencies herein. This book is not intended to provide legal, financial, or other professional advice.

TABLE OF CONTENT

CHAPTER 1

breed history

What is a Maltese?

The Maltese is a small, toy breed that has long captured the hearts of dog lovers worldwide. Known for its luxurious white coat and playful, affectionate demeanor, the Maltese is often considered an ideal companion dog. Despite their delicate appearance, they are a hardy and lively breed, full of energy and love for human companionship.

Standing at a height of 7 to 9 inches (17 to 23 cm) and weighing between 4 to 7 pounds (2 to 3 kg), the Maltese is one of the smallest dog breeds. They have a compact body, with a distinctive long, flowing, silky coat that covers them from head to toe. Unlike many other breeds, the Maltese does not shed much, making them an excellent choice for people with allergies. However, their coat requires regular grooming to maintain its beauty and prevent matting.

Despite their small size, Maltese dogs are known for their bold personality. They are confident, often standing their ground when faced with larger dogs or unfamiliar situations. Yet, they are not aggressive, and their nature is typically affectionate and gentle, making them great companions for individuals and families alike.

History of the Maltese

The Maltese is one of the oldest toy breeds in existence, with a history that spans several thousand years. The breed is believed to have originated in the Mediterranean region, and more specifically, the island of Malta. This location is thought to have given the breed its name, though there is some debate about whether the breed's origins trace back to other parts of the Mediterranean, such as Italy or Egypt.

Ancient depictions of small, long-haired dogs similar to the Maltese have been found in art and artifacts dating back over 2,000 years. These dogs were highly prized by the upper classes of society, often seen as a status symbol and cherished as pets by the nobility and royalty. The breed was so beloved that they were often depicted in paintings, tapestries, and sculptures alongside their owners.

Notably, the Maltese was a favored companion among many historical figures. In ancient Greece, for example, Maltese-like dogs were so revered that they were even given tombs to honor their passing. The Roman Empire also held the Maltese in high regard, with the breed appearing in works of Roman poetry and literature. Later, during the Renaissance, the breed found favor among European nobility. Queen Elizabeth I, Mary Queen of Scots, and the French Queen Marie Antoinette were all known to have owned Maltese dogs.

As trade routes expanded in the Middle Ages, the Maltese spread across Europe and into Asia. The breed's popularity grew steadily over the centuries, thanks in large part to its adaptability as a lapdog and its suitability for indoor living. By the 19th century, the Maltese had become a fixture in dog shows across Europe, and its reputation as a charming companion dog was firmly established.

The breed was introduced to the United States in the late 1800s and was officially recognized by the American Kennel Club (AKC) in 1888. Today, the Maltese continues to be a beloved pet around the world, admired for its beauty, intelligence, and unwavering devotion to its owners.

Physical Characteristics

The Maltese is renowned for its striking appearance, particularly its long, flowing white coat. This coat is its most defining feature and often sets it apart from other toy breeds. The hair is straight and silky, hanging gracefully to the ground, giving the dog a regal appearance. Despite the elegance of their coat, it requires significant maintenance to keep it clean and free of tangles or mats.

Their coat, Maltese dogs have a round skull with dark, expressive eyes that convey intelligence and alertness. Their ears are set low and close to the head, often blending in with their long fur, and they have a slightly rounded muzzle. Their nose is black and button-like, which adds to their overall cuteness. Their tail is carried gracefully over their back, adding to their elegant posture.

The Maltese has a compact and well-proportioned body. Their bones are fine, but they are not as fragile as they may appear. This breed is surprisingly sturdy and agile, capable of engaging in playful activities with enthusiasm.

Because of their luxurious coat, Maltese dogs often appear larger than they are, but underneath all that hair is a small, lightweight dog that can easily be carried or travel in a small carrier.

Typical Breed Behavior

Maltese dogs are known for their affectionate, friendly, and gentle temperament. They thrive on human companionship and are happiest when they are with their family, often following their owners from room to room. Despite their small size, Maltese are known for their lively and spirited personality. They are confident little dogs who are not afraid to engage with the world around them. This confidence, however, never crosses into aggression. Maltese dogs are generally friendly toward strangers, though they can be a little reserved when meeting new people.

Due to their intelligence, Maltese dogs are relatively easy to train. They are quick learners who respond well to positive reinforcement, such as treats and praise. Training them should focus on consistency and patience, as they can sometimes be a bit stubborn. It is important to start socialization early to ensure that they are well-adjusted and comfortable in various situations.

The Maltese is also known for being alert and vocal. They make excellent watchdogs, often barking at unfamiliar sounds or people approaching their home. While this trait makes them good at alerting their owners to potential dangers, it can also be problematic if not properly managed. Early training to curb excessive barking is often necessary.

Another characteristic of the Maltese is their playful nature. They are highly energetic and enjoy playtime, whether it is chasing a toy or engaging in interactive games with their owners. While they are small, they still require regular exercise to maintain their health and happiness. Short walks and indoor play sessions are usually sufficient to keep them content.

Overall, the Maltese is a highly adaptable breed that does well in various living situations. Whether in a small apartment or a larger home, they thrive as long as they receive enough attention and care. Their social nature and affectionate temperament make them excellent companions for individuals, couples, and families alike.

Is the Maltese the Right Dog for You?

Before deciding if a Maltese is the right dog for you, it is essential to consider several factors. While they are affectionate and charming pets, they also come with specific needs that must be met to ensure their happiness and health.

One of the most important things to consider is their grooming requirements. Maltese dogs have a high-maintenance coat that needs daily brushing to prevent tangles and mats. If you are not prepared to invest time in grooming or pay for professional grooming services, this breed may not be the best fit for you. However, their low-shedding coat can be a great advantage for those with allergies.

Maltese dogs also require a lot of attention and companionship. They are known for being "velcro dogs," meaning they form strong bonds with their owners and often want to be near them at all times. If you have a busy lifestyle that keeps you away from home for long periods, a Maltese may not be the best choice, as they can suffer from separation anxiety. On the other hand, if you are looking for a devoted companion who enjoys spending time with you, the Maltese could be the perfect match.

Another aspect to consider is their small size and fragility. While they are sturdy for their size, Maltese dogs are still small and can be easily injured if handled roughly or if they fall from a height. Families with young children need to be especially careful to ensure that the dog is treated gently. That said, their small size also makes them an excellent choice for people living in apartments or homes with limited space.

While Maltese dogs are generally friendly, they can sometimes be shy or cautious around strangers or new environments. Early socialization and positive experiences can help them become more confident in different situations.

The Maltese can be an excellent companion for the right owner. If you are willing to invest time in grooming, enjoy having a constant companion, and are prepared for their energy and need for attention, the Maltese could be the perfect addition to your life. However, if you prefer a more independent dog or are not able to commit to their grooming and care needs, you may want to consider other breeds.

CHAPTER 2

Choosing Your Maltese

Choosing a Maltese, whether through adoption or buying from a breeder, is an important decision that requires careful consideration. There are many factors to weigh, such as where you get your dog, the reputation of the breeder or rescue organization, and ensuring that the Maltese puppy you bring home fits your lifestyle. This chapter will guide you through the process of choosing your Maltese and making sure that both you and your new furry friend are set up for a long, happy relationship.

Buying Vs. Adopting

One of the first decisions you'll need to make when choosing a Maltese is whether to buy from a breeder or adopt from a rescue or shelter. Both options come with advantages and challenges, and the choice depends largely on your personal preferences and circumstances.

Buying from a Breeder

When you buy a Maltese from a breeder, you're more likely to get a purebred dog with known lineage, temperament, and health background. Reputable breeders will have documented pedigrees and may provide health guarantees, ensuring that you are purchasing a dog with fewer genetic health risks. Buying from a breeder also allows you to meet the puppy's parents, which can give you insight into what your dog will be like as an adult, both in terms of appearance and personality.

However, purchasing from a breeder typically comes with a higher price tag, especially for high-quality show or companion Maltese dogs. Breeders may charge anywhere from $1,000 to $4,000 or more, depending on the quality of the bloodline, location, and demand. If you're looking for a specific type of Maltese with particular traits, a breeder may be the best option.

Adopting from a Shelter or Rescue

Adopting a Maltese from a shelter or rescue organization can be a rewarding experience, and it often comes with a lower financial cost compared to purchasing from a breeder. Rescue organizations and shelters typically charge adoption fees ranging from $100 to $500, which covers veterinary care, vaccinations, and sometimes spaying or neutering. When you adopt, you're also giving a dog a second chance at a loving home, which can be incredibly fulfilling.

That said, adopting may come with fewer guarantees. In some cases, the dog's history, including health or temperament issues, may not be fully known. Additionally, rescue organizations often have older dogs available rather than puppies. While this can be a benefit for those looking to skip the challenges of raising a puppy, it may not suit everyone's preferences.

The Difference Between Animal Shelters and Rescue Organizations

Understanding the differences between animal shelters and rescue organizations is important when considering adoption. Each offers a different experience and may impact your adoption process.

Animal Shelters

Animal shelters are typically run by local governments or nonprofits, and they take in all kinds of animals, including stray or surrendered dogs. Shelters often have a wide variety of breeds and mixed-breed dogs, including Maltese, but availability can vary. These facilities tend to be high-volume, meaning they may have limited resources to assess the individual needs and behaviors of each dog.

Because shelters are often overcrowded, they may have a more urgent need to place dogs in homes. This can sometimes mean less detailed information on the dog's history, but it also means that adopting from a shelter is often quicker and easier than through other channels.

Rescue Organizations

Rescue organizations, on the other hand, tend to focus on specific breeds or types of dogs. Maltese rescue organizations exist across the country and specialize in rehabilitating and rehoming Maltese dogs in need. These organizations often operate on a smaller scale than shelters and are typically volunteer-run.

One of the main advantages of adopting from a rescue organization is that they usually place dogs in foster homes before they are adopted out. This allows the dogs to live in a home environment where their behavior and needs can be better assessed. Rescue organizations often provide more detailed information about the dog's temperament, health, and how they interact with people and other pets.

Rescue organizations may have stricter adoption processes, including home checks, interviews, and application reviews, but these measures are in place to ensure that the dogs go to a loving, suitable home.

Tips for Adopting a Maltese

If you decide to adopt a Maltese, here are some tips to help ensure the process goes smoothly:

1. **Research Breed-Specific Rescues**: Many breed-specific rescues, including those focused on Maltese, exist. These rescues understand the specific needs and characteristics of the breed and often have Maltese of all ages available for adoption.

2. **Ask About the Dog's History**: While the full history of an adopted dog may not always be available, try to get as much information as possible. Ask about any behavioral or medical issues the dog may have faced and what kind of environment the dog has been in previously.

3. **Be Patient**: The adoption process can take time. Some rescue organizations have waiting lists, and the process might include home visits or interviews. Patience is key, as the right dog for you will come along.

4. **Consider an Older Dog**: Puppies are often in high demand, but don't overlook older dogs. An adult or senior Maltese may already be

house-trained and less prone to the mischief that puppies can get into.

5. **Meet the Dog First**: Before making a commitment, it's always best to meet the dog to ensure their personality and energy level fit with your lifestyle.

Importance of Breeder Reputation

If you decide to purchase a Maltese from a breeder, the reputation of the breeder is one of the most critical factors to consider. A reputable breeder will prioritize the health and well-being of their dogs, ensuring that puppies are raised in a loving, safe, and clean environment.

Why Breeder Reputation Matters

Buying from a reputable breeder increases your chances of getting a healthy and well-adjusted puppy. Reputable breeders focus on maintaining breed standards, which includes breeding for good temperament, health, and conformation. In contrast, disreputable breeders, often called "backyard breeders" or "puppy mills," may prioritize profit over the health and care of the dogs. This can result in puppies with health issues, genetic disorders, or poor socialization.

A good breeder will provide detailed records of the puppy's lineage and health history. They will also offer support and advice even after the puppy goes home with you, as they genuinely care about the long-term welfare of their dogs.

Finding the Right Breeder

Finding a responsible breeder may take some time, but it's well worth the effort. Here are some tips to guide you:

1. **Do Your Research**: Start by researching breeders online and through breed clubs. The American Maltese Association (AMA) can be a valuable resource, as they often have breeder directories.
2. **Visit the Breeder's Facility**: A reputable breeder will invite you to visit their facility so you can see where the puppies are raised. The environment should be clean, and the dogs should appear healthy and happy.
3. **Ask for Health Screenings**: A responsible breeder will provide health clearances for the puppy's parents, ensuring that they have been screened for common genetic health issues. In the case of Maltese dogs, this may include testing for patellar luxation and heart conditions.

4. **Interview the Breeder**: A good breeder will ask you questions to ensure that you are a suitable owner for one of their puppies. They will want to know about your living situation, experience with dogs, and how you plan to care for the puppy.

Breeder Contracts and Guarantees

When buying a Maltese from a breeder, you should expect to sign a contract that outlines the terms of sale. This contract often includes details on health guarantees, the return policy, and spay/neuter agreements.

Health Guarantees

Many reputable breeders offer health guarantees, which typically cover genetic conditions that may arise in the first few years of the dog's life. This guarantees that the puppy is in good health at the time of sale and has been checked by a vet. If any hereditary conditions appear, the breeder may offer a replacement puppy or partial refund, depending on the contract terms.

Return Policy

A good breeder will also include a return policy in the contract. This ensures that if, for any reason, you can no longer care for the dog, the breeder will take the dog back or help find a new home. This is important, as it shows the breeder's commitment to the dog's well-being throughout its life.

Picking the Perfect Puppy

When it comes time to pick your Maltese puppy, it's important to choose one that fits your lifestyle and personality. Even within the same litter, puppies can have different temperaments and energy levels.

The Different Puppy Personality Types

1. **The Confident Puppy**: This puppy is bold, curious, and eager to explore. They tend to be leaders and may be more independent. If you want a dog that is confident and outgoing, this may be the right fit for you.
2. **The Calm Puppy**: Some puppies are naturally more laid-back and relaxed. They may be content to sit back and watch while their siblings play. A calm puppy is often a good choice for someone looking for a quieter, more relaxed companion.
3. **The Playful Puppy**: Puppies with a playful personality are always ready for fun. They love to interact with people and other dogs, making them ideal for active households.
4. **The Shy Puppy**: Shy puppies may take a little more time to warm up to new people and

environments, but with patience and socialization, they can become affectionate and loyal companions.

By observing the puppies and interacting with them, you can get a sense of their personalities and choose the one that will best fit your home. Whether you opt for a confident, playful, or calm puppy, the most important thing is to ensure they are well-socialized, healthy, and come from a responsible source.

Choosing a Maltese is an exciting journey, and whether you adopt or buy, taking the time to make informed decisions will ensure a happy and fulfilling life with your new companion.

CHAPTER 3

Preparing for Your Maltese

Bringing a new Maltese into your home is an exciting time, but it also requires preparation to ensure a smooth transition for your new pet. Whether it's creating a safe space for your dog, introducing them to children or other pets, or gathering all the necessary supplies, preparing adequately will help your Maltese settle in more comfortably and reduce potential issues. This chapter will provide a comprehensive guide to getting your home ready for your new Maltese, from puppy-proofing to preparing both indoor and outdoor spaces.

Preparing Children and Other Pets

One of the most important steps in preparing for a new Maltese is ensuring that your family is ready, especially if you have children or other pets. Maltese dogs are known for their gentle and affectionate nature, but introducing them to new environments and companions requires careful planning.

Preparing Children

Maltese dogs are small and delicate, which means children, particularly younger ones, must learn how to interact with them properly. Teaching your children the appropriate way to handle and play with the new puppy is key to ensuring the safety of both your Maltese and your child.

1. **Gentle Handling**: Teach children to be gentle when touching or picking up the Maltese. They should never pull on the dog's ears, tail, or fur. Because Maltese dogs are small, rough handling can easily injure them.

2. **Respecting Boundaries**: Explain to children that dogs, like people, need their own space. Children should learn to recognize signs that the puppy is tired, scared, or needs alone time, such as backing away, whining, or hiding. Maltese are friendly dogs, but they can get overwhelmed if over handled.

3. **Supervised Play**: Until your Maltese and children have established a strong bond, it's best to supervise all interactions. This ensures that both the puppy and the children learn how to play and interact positively.

4. **Teaching Responsibility**: Involving your children in caring for the new Maltese can help foster responsibility. Simple tasks like feeding or brushing the dog, under your supervision, can

give children a sense of involvement and help create a bond between them and the puppy.

Preparing Other Pets

Introducing a new Maltese to a household with existing pets, whether they are dogs, cats, or other animals, must be done gradually to avoid tension and to help everyone adjust smoothly.

1. **Slow Introductions**: The first meeting between your new Maltese and your other pets should be done in a controlled, calm environment. Use leashes or crates if necessary to keep the animals calm. Let them sniff each other from a distance and observe their reactions before allowing closer contact.
2. **Separate Spaces**: It's wise to give each pet their own space initially, especially during the first few days. This allows your new Maltese to explore their new home without feeling overwhelmed and gives existing pets time to adjust to the new presence.
3. **Monitor for Jealousy**: Your other pets may feel jealous or threatened by the new addition, so give your existing pets plenty of attention and maintain their regular routines. This will reassure them that the new Maltese isn't taking their place.

4. **Positive Reinforcement**: Reward all pets with treats and praise for positive interactions. This helps reinforce good behavior and creates positive associations between your existing pets and the new Maltese.

Puppy-Proofing Your Home

Maltese puppies are curious and playful, which means they may get into trouble if your home isn't properly puppy-proofed. Much like baby-proofing, you'll need to assess your home for potential hazards and make it a safe environment for your new dog.

General Areas

1. **Remove Small Objects**: Maltese puppies may be tempted to chew or swallow small objects such as coins, paperclips, or jewelry. Keep these items out of reach to prevent choking or intestinal blockages.
2. **Secure Electrical Cords**: Puppies often find electrical cords appealing for chewing. Use cord protectors or keep cords out of reach to prevent electrocution or burns.
3. **Block Off Unsafe Areas**: Use baby gates to block off rooms or stairways that may be dangerous for your puppy. Maltese puppies,

being small, may also slip through railings or gaps in stairs, so ensure these areas are secure.

4. **Keep Floors Clean**: Maltese puppies may chew on or ingest anything they find on the floor, so keeping floors free of clutter, small toys, or trash is important for their safety.

Living Room

1. **Protect Furniture**: Maltese puppies may chew on furniture, especially while teething. Use bitter spray deterrents on furniture legs or use barriers to prevent access to valuable or delicate pieces.

2. **Be Mindful of Houseplants**: Some houseplants are toxic to dogs. Remove plants such as philodendrons, lilies, and poinsettias, or place them in areas that your Maltese cannot reach.

3. **Rugs and Carpeting**: Puppies are likely to have accidents as they learn to be house-trained. Consider rolling up expensive rugs or using washable mats in high-traffic areas where your Maltese will spend time.

Dangerous Things Your Dog Might Eat

One of the biggest dangers to a new puppy in the home is the risk of ingesting harmful items. While Maltese are small, their curiosity knows no bounds, and they may try to chew on or eat things that are unsafe. Being aware of common household hazards can help prevent accidents.

Toxic Foods

Some foods that are safe for humans can be toxic to dogs, including:

1. **Chocolate**: Even a small amount of chocolate can be toxic to dogs. Dark chocolate and baking chocolate are particularly dangerous due to their high levels of theobromine.
2. **Grapes and Raisins**: Grapes and raisins can cause kidney failure in dogs. Even a few can lead to severe health issues.
3. **Onions and Garlic**: These foods contain compounds that can damage a dog's red blood cells, leading to anemia.
4. **Xylitol**: This artificial sweetener, often found in sugar-free gum and candy, can cause a dangerous drop in blood sugar levels in dogs.

Household Chemicals

1. **Cleaning Products**: Many household cleaners contain chemicals that are harmful if ingested or come into contact with your dog's skin. Keep all cleaning products locked away or out of reach.

2. **Pesticides and Fertilizers**: Lawn and garden chemicals, such as pesticides, herbicides, and fertilizers, can be dangerous if your Maltese ingests or comes into contact with them. Always store these chemicals in a secure place.
3. **Medications**: Human medications, such as pain relievers, cold medications, and vitamins, should never be left where a dog can access them. Even small amounts can be toxic.

Supplies to Purchase Before You Bring Your Maltese Home

Before bringing your Maltese home, it's essential to have the right supplies on hand to ensure their comfort and safety. Here's a list of items to purchase:

1. **Dog Crate**: A crate provides your Maltese with a safe, secure place to rest and helps with house-training. Choose a crate size appropriate for small dogs, with enough space for your Maltese to stand, turn around, and lie down comfortably.
2. **Bedding**: Soft, comfortable bedding is important for your Maltese's crate or designated sleeping area. Look for washable beds or mats that can be easily cleaned.

3. **Food and Water Bowls**: Stainless steel or ceramic bowls are ideal, as they are durable and easy to clean. Avoid plastic bowls, as they can harbor bacteria and cause allergic reactions in some dogs.

4. **Puppy Food**: Choose high-quality puppy food that meets the nutritional needs of small breeds. Your breeder or veterinarian can recommend specific brands suited for Maltese puppies.

5. **Collar and Leash**: A lightweight collar and leash are essential for walks and outings. Make sure the collar is adjustable and fits snugly without being too tight.

6. **Toys**: Maltese puppies need toys to keep them entertained and stimulated. Choose chew toys, plush toys, and interactive toys that are safe for small dogs.

7. **Grooming Supplies**: Maltese dogs require regular grooming, so invest in a good-quality brush, nail clippers, and dog shampoo. A detangling spray can help keep their coats smooth and free of mats.

8. **Pee Pads**: While house-training, pee pads can help contain accidents, especially if you live in an apartment or cannot take your puppy outside frequently.

Preparing an Indoor Space

Your Maltese will spend most of its time indoors, so creating a comfortable and safe space is essential. Designate an area in your home for your dog to relax, play, and sleep.

Safe Zone

Create a "safe zone" where your puppy can rest undisturbed. This could be a crate or a small, enclosed area with a bed, toys, and access to food and water. This space will become a retreat for your Maltese when they need to rest or feel overwhelmed.

Temperature Control

Maltese dogs are small and can be sensitive to temperature changes. Make sure the indoor space is neither too hot nor too cold, and avoid placing their bed in drafty areas or directly in front of heating vents.

Cleanliness

Maltese dogs have long, white coats that can get dirty easily. Keep their indoor space clean by regularly washing their bedding and vacuuming to remove hair and dirt. Clean the food and water bowls daily to prevent bacteria buildup.

Preparing an Outdoor Space

While Maltese dogs are primarily indoor pets, they still need time outdoors for exercise and fresh air. Preparing a safe outdoor space is important for your dog's physical and mental well-being.

Fenced Yard

If you have a yard, ensure it is securely fenced to prevent your Maltese from escaping. Because of their small size, they can slip through small gaps or under gates. Regularly inspect the fence for weak spots and make necessary repairs.

Supervision

Never leave your Maltese unattended outdoors, especially in extreme weather conditions. Due to their small size, they are vulnerable to predators such as hawks, coyotes, and even larger dogs. Always supervise their outdoor playtime.

Shade and Shelter

If your Maltese spends time outside, provide a shaded area where they can rest away from the sun. During colder months, limit outdoor time, as their small size makes them more susceptible to cold temperatures.

By taking the time to prepare your home and outdoor space for your Maltese, you ensure that your new companion will have a safe, comfortable environment where they can thrive.

CHAPTER 4

Bringing Home Your Maltese

Bringing home a new Maltese puppy is a moment filled with excitement and joy, but it also comes with responsibilities. The transition from breeder or shelter to your home can be overwhelming for a puppy, and it's important to make the process as smooth as possible. This chapter will guide you through the steps of picking up your Maltese, how to manage the ride home, what to expect during the first night, the importance of the first vet visit, and an overview of the costs involved in owning a Maltese.

Picking Up Your Maltese

The day you pick up your new Maltese is a special one, but it can also be stressful for both you and the puppy. Before heading out, ensure you have all the necessary items to make the trip comfortable and safe for your new dog.

What to Bring

1. **Crate or Carrier**: Bring a small crate or carrier for the car ride. A crate helps to keep your Maltese safe and secure during the drive, preventing them from moving around the car and possibly distracting the driver. Make sure the crate is large enough for the puppy to turn around and lie down but small enough to feel cozy and secure.
2. **Blanket or Towel**: Bring a soft blanket or towel to place inside the crate. If possible, ask the breeder or shelter for an item that smells like the puppy's mother or littermates to help comfort them during the trip home.
3. **Water and Bowl**: If you're traveling a long distance, bring some water and a small bowl in case your Maltese needs a drink along the way.
4. **Toys or Chew Items**: A small toy or chew item can help keep the puppy occupied during the ride home.

Picking Up the Puppy

When you arrive to pick up your Maltese, there are a few things to keep in mind to ensure the transition goes smoothly.

1. **Talk to the Breeder or Shelter Staff**: Before leaving, talk to the breeder or shelter staff about your puppy's current feeding schedule, any

vaccinations or treatments they've had, and any other important information. It's also a good idea to get a copy of the puppy's health records and pedigree if available.

2. **Keep It Calm**: While you may be excited to meet your new puppy, remember that this is a big change for them. Keep your voice and movements calm to avoid overwhelming them.

3. **First Bonding Moment**: Spend a few minutes holding or petting your Maltese before placing them in the crate. This will help them associate your presence with comfort and security, making the transition to your home easier.

The Ride Home

The ride home is often the first time your Maltese will be separated from its mother and littermates, and this can be a confusing and frightening experience for the puppy. Here are a few tips to make the journey as stress-free as possible.

Keeping the Puppy Calm

Your Maltese may whine or cry during the car ride because they're scared and unsure of what's happening. This is normal, and with a little patience, they'll soon settle down.

1. **Stay Calm**: If your puppy starts crying, resist the urge to open the crate or take them out. Instead, talk to them in a calm and reassuring voice. Remember, the car ride is a new experience, and your calm demeanor will help them feel more at ease.
2. **Avoid Sudden Movements**: Try to drive smoothly and avoid sudden stops or turns, as these can be unsettling for a small puppy.
3. **Take Breaks**: If you're traveling a long distance, take a few breaks to allow the puppy to stretch, relieve themselves, and have a drink of water. Always keep the puppy on a leash when outside the car to prevent them from running off.
4. **Music and Sounds**: Some puppies find the sounds of soft music or white noise calming during car rides. You can play gentle music at a low volume to help soothe your Maltese.

The First Night

The first night in a new home can be one of the most challenging moments for both you and your Maltese. This is often the first time the puppy is away from its mother and littermates, and the new surroundings can feel unfamiliar and overwhelming.

Preparing a Sleeping Area

To help your Maltese settle in for the night, prepare a comfortable and secure sleeping area before bringing them home.

1. **Crate Training**: Many experts recommend crate training as it provides your puppy with a safe, den-like space where they can feel secure. Place the crate in a quiet, warm area of the house, such as your bedroom or a quiet corner of the living room. This way, your puppy won't feel too isolated or alone.
2. **Bedding**: Use soft bedding inside the crate to make it comfortable. As mentioned earlier, placing a blanket or item that smells like the puppy's mother can provide comfort.
3. **Nighttime Routine**: Establishing a nighttime routine can help your Maltese adjust more quickly. Take your puppy outside to relieve themselves right before bed, then place them in the crate with a chew toy or soft toy for comfort.

Handling Nighttime Whining

It's common for puppies to whine or cry during the first few nights. This is often because they miss the comfort of their mother and littermates. While it can be difficult to hear, it's important to remain patient and not rush to comfort the puppy immediately.

1. **Ignore Whining (At First)**: If your Maltese starts whining, give them a few minutes to settle down on their own. Rushing in to comfort them may reinforce the behavior, teaching the puppy that whining gets attention.
2. **Provide Comfort**: If the whining persists and you believe the puppy needs to relieve themselves, take them outside briefly but avoid making it a playtime experience. Afterward, return the puppy to their crate and encourage them to go back to sleep.
3. **Patience Is Key**: It may take a few nights for your Maltese to fully adjust to their new sleeping environment. With time and consistency, they will begin to feel more secure and sleep through the night.

The First Vet Visit

One of the first things you should do after bringing your Maltese home is schedule a visit to the veterinarian. This initial vet visit is crucial for ensuring your puppy is healthy and starting their journey toward a long, happy life.

What to Expect

During your Maltese's first vet visit, the veterinarian will conduct a thorough health check to assess your puppy's overall well-being.

1. **Physical Examination**: The vet will check your puppy's ears, eyes, mouth, skin, and overall body condition to ensure they are healthy. They'll also listen to the puppy's heart and lungs to check for any abnormalities.
2. **Vaccinations**: If your puppy hasn't already received their first set of vaccinations, the vet will begin a vaccination schedule to protect against common diseases like distemper, parvovirus, and rabies.
3. **Parasite Prevention**: Your vet will check for signs of parasites such as fleas, ticks, or intestinal worms and may recommend preventive treatments such as flea medication or deworming.
4. **Microchipping**: If your Maltese hasn't been microchipped, this is an excellent time to have the procedure done. Microchipping provides permanent identification, helping to reunite you with your puppy if they ever get lost.

Questions to Ask

The first vet visit is also an opportunity to ask questions about your Maltese's health and care needs.

1. **Feeding Guidelines**: Ask your vet for recommendations on the best diet for your Maltese puppy, including portion sizes and feeding frequency.
2. **Growth and Development**: Inquire about your puppy's expected growth rate and any milestones to watch for in the coming weeks and months.
3. **Spaying or Neutering**: Ask your vet about the appropriate time to spay or neuter your Maltese, and discuss the benefits of the procedure.

The Cost of Ownership

Owning a Maltese is a long-term financial commitment, and it's important to be aware of the costs involved before bringing your puppy home. Understanding these costs can help you budget and ensure you're prepared to meet your Maltese's needs throughout their life.

Initial Costs

1. **Purchase Price**: Depending on whether you buy from a breeder or adopt from a shelter, the initial cost of acquiring a Maltese can vary significantly. Purebred Maltese puppies from reputable breeders typically range from $1,000 to $3,000, while adoption fees from shelters or rescue

organizations are usually much lower, around $100 to $500.

2. **Vet Visits and Vaccinations**: Initial vet visits, vaccinations, and preventive care can add up to several hundred dollars. Expect to spend around $200 to $500 during the first few months for vaccinations, deworming, and microchipping.

3. **Supplies**: The cost of supplies, including a crate, bedding, food, toys, grooming tools, and bowls, will range from $200 to $400. Some of these items are one-time purchases, while others, such as food and grooming supplies, will need to be replenished regularly.

Ongoing Costs

1. **Food**: High-quality dog food for a Maltese will typically cost around $20 to $50 per month, depending on the brand and whether you choose to feed dry kibble, wet food, or a mix of both.

2. **Grooming**: Maltese dogs require regular grooming to maintain their coat and overall hygiene. Professional grooming sessions every 4 to 6 weeks can cost between $40 and $100 per visit. Alternatively, grooming at home can help reduce costs but requires an investment in grooming tools and training.

3. **Health Care**: Routine vet visits, preventive medications (such as flea, tick, and heartworm preventives), and any unexpected health issues can cost several hundred dollars per year. It's also wise to consider pet insurance, which can help offset the cost of major medical expenses.
4. **Training and Socialization**: Puppy training classes or professional behavior training may be necessary, especially if your Maltese needs help with basic obedience or socialization. Expect to spend between $100 and $300 on training during the first year.

By being prepared for the financial responsibilities that come with owning a Maltese, you can ensure that your new companion receives the best care possible throughout their life.

CHAPTER 5

Being a Puppy Parent

Becoming a puppy parent is a rewarding experience, but it also comes with its challenges. Your Maltese, like all puppies, will require patience, understanding, and time as they learn to adjust to their new environment and develop good behavior. This chapter will guide you through what it means to be a responsible puppy parent, including having realistic expectations, dealing with common puppy behaviors such as chewing, digging, barking, and growling, and addressing issues like heel nipping and separation anxiety. Additionally, we'll cover the basics of crate training and how to leave your puppy home alone safely.

Have Realistic Expectations

When bringing home a Maltese puppy, it's important to set realistic expectations about the time, effort, and patience needed to raise a well-adjusted dog. Puppies are a lot like babies in that they need constant care, training, and supervision, especially in their first few months of life. They will make mistakes, and you may find yourself frustrated at times, but with the right approach and realistic expectations, you can build a strong bond and develop a well-behaved dog.

Puppies Need Time to Learn

Puppies are not born knowing what is right or wrong. They will need time to learn proper behavior, and it's essential to remember that they will make mistakes along the way. Potty training, for example, can take several weeks or even months, depending on your puppy's learning curve and how consistent you are with their training.

Patience is Key

As a puppy parent, you will need to exercise patience. Puppies are curious and easily distracted, and sometimes it can feel like they are testing your limits. However, yelling or punishing a puppy is counterproductive and can damage the trust you're building with them. Instead, focus on positive reinforcement, rewarding good behavior with treats, praise, and playtime. Over time, your puppy will begin to understand what is expected of them.

Chewing

One of the most common behaviors that new puppy parents encounter is chewing. Puppies explore the world with their mouths, and they will chew on anything they can find—from shoes to furniture. Chewing is also a natural behavior for puppies because it helps relieve the discomfort of teething.

How to Handle Chewing

1. **Provide Chew Toys**: One of the best ways to prevent destructive chewing is to give your Maltese appropriate chew toys. Rubber toys, dental chews, and rope toys are great options for teething puppies. Keep a variety of toys available to keep your puppy entertained.

2. **Puppy-Proof Your Home**: Keep items that your puppy might be tempted to chew, such as shoes, books, and remote controls, out of reach. This will minimize the chances of destructive chewing and protect your belongings.

3. **Redirect the Behavior**: If you catch your Maltese chewing on something inappropriate, calmly redirect them to a toy or chew item. Praise them when they start chewing the appropriate item.

4. **Crate Training**: When you're not able to supervise your puppy, using a crate can help prevent destructive chewing. Make sure to place

a chew toy or two in the crate to keep your puppy entertained.

Digging

Digging is another natural behavior for puppies, especially if they are bored, anxious, or trying to escape from a confined space. Maltese dogs are not typically known for excessive digging, but it can still happen from time to time.

How to Handle Digging

1. **Provide Mental and Physical Stimulation**: One of the main reasons puppy dogs are out of boredom. Make sure your Maltese is getting enough physical exercise and mental stimulation through playtime, walks, and training sessions.
2. **Create a Designated Digging Area**: If your puppy enjoys digging, consider setting up a designated digging spot in the yard where it's okay for them to dig. You can bury toys or treats in the designated area to encourage them to dig there instead of in other parts of the yard.
3. **Supervise Outdoor Time**: If your puppy starts digging in areas where they shouldn't, such as flower beds or under fences, redirect their attention with toys or games.

4. **Address Anxiety**: If your puppy is digging because of anxiety, such as trying to escape from the yard, address the root cause of the anxiety. This may involve gradually acclimating them to being alone or using crate training.

Barking and Growling

Barking and growling are natural forms of communication for dogs, but excessive barking or growling can become a problem if not addressed early on. Maltese dogs, being alert and lively, may be prone to barking at strangers or unusual noises, but with proper training, you can teach them when it's appropriate to bark.

How to Handle Barking and Growling

1. **Identify the Cause**: Puppies bark or growl for many reasons, including fear, excitement, or to get attention. The first step in addressing excessive barking or growling is to identify the cause. Are they barking at the doorbell, other dogs, or when left alone?

2. **Teach the 'Quiet' Command**: One effective way to manage barking is to teach your puppy the 'quiet' command. When your Maltese barks, say 'quiet' in a firm but calm voice. When they

stop barking, reward them with praise or a treat. Consistency is key in reinforcing this behavior.

3. **Desensitization**: If your Maltese is barking out of fear or excitement, such as at visitors or other dogs, gradually expose them to the trigger in a controlled manner. Over time, they will learn that the trigger is not something to be afraid of or overly excited about.

4. **Avoid Punishment**: Never yell at or punish your puppy for barking or growling, as this can increase anxiety and make the behavior worse. Instead, focus on positive reinforcement and redirection.

Heel Nipping

Heel nipping is a common behavior in puppies, especially in breeds that have a herding instinct. While Maltese dogs are not herding dogs, they may still engage in heel nipping during play or when they are excited.

How to Handle Heel Nipping

1. **Redirect the Behavior**: If your puppy starts nipping at your heels, immediately stop walking and redirect their attention to a toy or another activity. This teaches them that nipping does not result in play or attention.

2. **Teach the 'Leave It' Command**: Teaching your Maltese the 'leave it' command can help stop unwanted behaviors like heel nipping. When your puppy starts to nip, say 'leave it' and offer a toy or treat as a distraction.
3. **Provide Plenty of Exercise**: Puppies often nip when they are full of energy. Make sure your Maltese is getting enough exercise and playtime to burn off excess energy and reduce the likelihood of nipping.
4. **Socialization**: Expose your puppy to other dogs and people so they learn appropriate ways to interact and play without resorting to nipping.

Separation Anxiety

Separation anxiety is a common issue in dogs, especially in breeds like the Maltese that are known for their strong attachment to their owners. Puppies with separation anxiety may become distressed when left alone, leading to behaviors like barking, whining, or destructive chewing.

How to Handle Separation Anxiety

1. **Gradual Departures**: When you first bring your Maltese home, practice leaving them alone for short periods of time and gradually increase the

duration. This helps them get used to being on their own without becoming anxious.

2. **Create a Safe Space**: Provide your puppy with a safe and comfortable space, such as a crate or a designated room, where they can feel secure when you're not home. Leave them with a favorite toy or blanket to help ease their anxiety.

3. **Ignore Excited Greetings**: When you return home, avoid making a big fuss over your puppy. Instead, wait until they are calm before giving them attention. This helps teach them that your departures and returns are not a big deal.

4. **Leave Comfort Items**: Leave items that smell like you, such as a worn T-shirt, in your puppy's crate or bed to provide comfort while you're gone.

Crate Training Basics

Crate training is a valuable tool for raising a well-behaved Maltese. A crate provides your puppy with a safe and secure space where they can relax, and it helps with potty training and preventing destructive behavior when you're not home.

How to Crate Train Your Maltese

1. **Introduce the Crate Gradually**: Start by introducing your Maltese to the crate in a positive way. Place treats, toys, or bedding inside the crate to make it inviting. Leave the door open at first so your puppy can explore the crate at their own pace.
2. **Use the Crate for Short Periods**: Begin by having your puppy spend short periods of time in the crate while you're home. Gradually increase the amount of time they spend in the crate, always rewarding them with treats or praise when they go in.
3. **Never Use the Crate as Punishment**: The crate should always be a positive and safe space for your puppy. Never use it as a form of punishment, as this can create fear and anxiety around the crate.
4. **Establish a Crate Routine**: Create a routine for using the crate, such as putting your Maltese in the crate during nap times or when you're away for short periods. This helps them get used to being in the crate and prevents separation anxiety.

Leaving Your Dog Home Alone

Leaving your Maltese home alone for the first time can be a daunting experience for both you and your puppy.

However, with proper preparation, you can help ease the transition and prevent anxiety or destructive behavior.

How to Leave Your Puppy Home Alone

1. **Practice Gradual Absences**: Just like with crate training, start by leaving your puppy alone for short periods and gradually increase the time you're away. This helps them adjust to being alone without becoming anxious.

2. **Create a Safe Environment**: Make sure your puppy is in a safe, secure space, such as a crate or a designated room, when you're not home. Remove any dangerous items they could chew on or get into, and provide toys or puzzles to keep them entertained.

3. **Provide Comfort Items**: Leaving a favorite toy, blanket, or an item that smells like you can provide comfort and help reduce separation anxiety.

4. **Exercise Before Leaving**: Make sure your puppy gets plenty of exercise before you leave, whether it's a walk or playtime. A tired puppy is less likely to become anxious or destructive while you're gone.

By understanding and addressing the common behaviors that come with being a puppy parent, you can raise a well-adjusted and happy Maltese. With patience, consistency, and love, your puppy will grow into a well-behaved companion that brings joy to your life.

CHAPTER 6

Potty Training Your Maltese

Potty training is one of the most important and sometimes challenging parts of being a new puppy parent. Maltese dogs, like many small breeds, can be a bit tricky to potty train due to their small bladders and independent personalities. However, with consistency, patience, and the right techniques, you can successfully potty train your Maltese. In this chapter, we'll explore different methods of potty training, how to use the crate for potty training, what to expect during the first few weeks, how to handle accidents, and the pros and cons of using doggy doors.

Methods of Potty Training

There are several methods of potty training that you can use with your Maltese. Choosing the right method will depend on your living situation, your puppy's personality, and your personal preferences. The most common methods are outdoor potty training, indoor potty training with pee pads, and using a litter box. Let's take a closer look at each.

Outdoor Potty Training

This is the traditional method where you take your puppy outside to eliminate. It is usually the preferred method for people with yards or easy access to outdoor spaces. The key to outdoor potty training is consistency—taking your puppy out at regular intervals and rewarding them for going in the right spot.

1. **Establish a Routine**: Start by taking your Maltese outside first thing in the morning, after meals, after naps, and before bed. Puppies have small bladders and may need to go every 1-2 hours during the day. Make sure to take them to the same spot each time so they can associate the area with potty time.
2. **Use a Command**: Choose a consistent command, such as "go potty," and use it each time you take your puppy outside. Over time, they will begin to associate the command with the act of elimination.
3. **Positive Reinforcement**: Immediately after your puppy goes potty in the right spot, reward them with praise, treats, or playtime. This positive reinforcement will help them understand that going outside is good behavior.

Indoor Potty Training with Pee Pads

For those who live in apartments or areas with harsh weather, indoor potty training with pee pads might be a better option. Pee pads can be used temporarily until your puppy is ready to transition to outdoor pottying, or they can be a permanent solution if outdoor access is limited.

1. **Choose a Designated Spot**: Place the pee pads in a specific area of your home where you want your puppy to go. Keep the spot consistent so that your puppy learns to associate it with potty time.
2. **Transitioning Outdoors**: If you eventually want your Maltese to go potty outside, start by moving the pee pad closer to the door over time. Once your puppy is used to going near the door, you can begin taking them outside instead of using the pad.
3. **Change Pads Regularly**: Keep the potty area clean by changing the pee pads frequently. Puppies are more likely to use the pads if the area is clean and free of odors.

Litter Box Training

Litter box training is another option, particularly for small dogs like the Maltese. This method is similar to pee pad training, but instead of pads, you use a small litter box filled with dog-safe litter. This method is ideal for owners who want to provide a permanent indoor potty solution.

1. **Introduce the Litter Box Early**: Start by placing your puppy in the litter box after meals, naps, and playtime. Use positive reinforcement when they use the box correctly.
2. **Choose the Right Litter**: Use a non-toxic, dog-safe litter that is comfortable for your puppy to walk on. Avoid clumping litters, as these can be harmful if ingested.
3. **Keep the Box Clean**: Like with pee pads, it's important to keep the litter box clean to encourage your puppy to use it consistently.

Using the Crate for Potty Training

Crate training is a powerful tool for potty training because it taps into your puppy's natural instinct to avoid soiling their sleeping area. When used correctly, a crate can help establish a routine and prevent accidents in the house.

How Crate Training Helps with Potty Training

1. **Encourages Holding It**: Puppies are naturally inclined to keep their sleeping area clean. By confining your Maltese to a crate that is just large enough for them to stand up, turn around, and lie

down, they will learn to "hold it" until they are let outside. This teaches bladder control and helps establish a potty routine.

2. **Prevents Accidents**: When you cannot supervise your puppy, keeping them in the crate reduces the chances of accidents in the house. Be sure not to leave them in the crate for too long, as puppies cannot hold their bladder for extended periods, especially when they are very young.

3. **Nighttime Training**: At night, your puppy will likely need to go out at least once or twice, depending on their age. By creating them near your bed, you can hear when they need to go out and take them outside. Over time, they will start sleeping through the night without needing a bathroom break.

Tips for Using a Crate for Potty Training

1. **Introduce the Crate Positively**: Make the crate a positive and comfortable space by adding soft bedding and toys. Use treats and praise to encourage your puppy to go inside willingly.

2. **Avoid Overusing the Crate**: While the crate is a useful tool for potty training, it should not be used as a place to keep your puppy for long periods of time. Puppies need plenty of playtime, socialization, and exercise outside of the crate.

3. **Create a Routine**: Take your puppy out of the crate at regular intervals to go potty. Make sure to take them out first thing in the morning, after meals, and before bed.

The First Few Weeks

The first few weeks of potty training are crucial in establishing good habits for your Maltese. During this time, it's important to be consistent, patient, and prepared for some accidents along the way.

What to Expect

1. **Frequent Potty Breaks**: During the first few weeks, your puppy will need to go outside or use the pee pad frequently. Expect to take them out every 1-2 hours, as well as after meals, naps, and playtime.
2. **Supervision is Key**: Keep a close eye on your puppy during this time, as they will likely show signs when they need to go, such as sniffing the ground, circling, or whining. If you see these behaviors, immediately take them to the designated potty area.
3. **Accidents Will Happen**: It's important to remember that accidents are a normal part of the potty training process. Stay calm and never

punish your puppy for having an accident. Instead, clean it up with an enzyme-based cleaner to remove the scent and prevent them from going in the same spot again.

4. **Consistency is Crucial**: Stick to a consistent routine during the first few weeks. Take your puppy out at the same times each day, use the same command, and reward them for going in the right spot. Consistency will help your Maltese learn faster and reduce the likelihood of accidents.

How to Handle Accidents

Accidents are an inevitable part of potty training, especially during the first few weeks. How you handle accidents can make a big difference in the success of your training efforts.

Steps for Handling Accidents

1. **Stay Calm**: If you catch your puppy in the act of having an accident, calmly pick them up and take them to the designated potty area. Do not yell or punish them, as this can cause fear and confusion.

2. **Praise for Correct Behavior**: If your puppy finishes going potty in the correct spot, praise

them and offer a treat. Positive reinforcement helps them understand where they should be going.

3. **Clean Thoroughly**: Use an enzyme-based cleaner to clean up accidents. This type of cleaner breaks down the proteins in urine, which helps eliminate the smell and reduces the likelihood of your puppy going in the same spot again.

4. **Reevaluate Your Routine**: If accidents are happening frequently, it may be a sign that you need to adjust your potty training routine. For example, you may need to take your puppy out more frequently or use a crate more often when you're not able to supervise.

Pros and Cons of Doggy Doors

Doggy doors can be a convenient option for potty training, especially if you have a yard and want to give your Maltese the freedom to go outside when they need to. However, there are both advantages and disadvantages to using a doggy door for potty training.

Pros of Doggy Doors

1. **Convenience**: Doggy doors allow your puppy to go outside to potty whenever they need to, which

can make potty training easier and reduce accidents inside the house.

2. **Independence**: With a doggy door, your Maltese can learn to be more independent and go outside without needing you to open the door for them every time.

3. **Flexibility**: If you're not always home or available to take your puppy out, a doggy door provides them with the flexibility to go outside on their own.

Cons of Doggy Doors

1. **Safety Concerns**: Doggy doors can pose a safety risk, especially if they are large enough for other animals or even people to enter your home. There is also the risk of your puppy escaping the yard if it is not securely fenced.

2. **Supervision Issues**: With a doggy door, your puppy may be able to go outside unsupervised, which can be dangerous if they get into something they shouldn't, such as toxic plants or harmful objects.

3. **Potential for Overuse**: Some puppies may overuse the doggy door, going in and out frequently, which can make it harder for them to learn a structured potty routine.

Potty training your Maltese requires patience, consistency, and a well-thought-out plan. By choosing the right method, using the crate effectively, and addressing accidents properly, you can help your puppy develop good potty habits and prevent accidents in the house.

CHAPTER 7

Socializing Your Maltese

Maltese dogs are known for their affectionate and gentle personalities. However, like all dogs, they require proper socialization to become well-mannered, confident, and happy in a variety of situations. In this chapter, we'll explore the importance of socialization, how to help your Maltese interact safely with other dogs and pets, tips for socializing adult dogs, and best practices for greeting new people. We'll also address specific guidance for Maltese dogs around children to ensure everyone stays safe and comfortable.

Importance of Socialization

Socialization is the process of exposing your Maltese to various environments, people, animals, sounds, and experiences to help them develop into a well-rounded, confident companion. This process is essential during puppyhood but remains important throughout their life.

Benefits of Socialization

1. **Reduces Fear and Anxiety**: Early and consistent socialization can help prevent your Maltese from developing fears or anxieties, which are common in small dog breeds.
2. **Promotes Positive Behavior**: Socialization helps your dog learn how to behave appropriately around others, reducing the likelihood of unwanted behaviors like excessive barking, snapping, or aggression.
3. **Increases Confidence**: A well-socialized Maltese feels more comfortable in new situations, whether it's meeting strangers, visiting the vet, or exploring new environments.
4. **Builds Stronger Bonds**: Socialization enhances your Maltese's trust in you as their owner and leader. This bond creates a stronger, happier relationship between you and your pet.

When to Start Socializing

It's ideal to begin socializing your Maltese between 8 and 16 weeks of age when they are most receptive to new experiences. This "socialization window" is critical for puppies as they are more open to learning and adapting to new situations. However, if you have an older Maltese who missed out on early socialization, don't worry—adult dogs can still be socialized with patience and positive reinforcement.

Behavior Around Other Dogs

Maltese dogs are generally friendly but can sometimes be cautious or even territorial around other dogs. Teaching them how to interact with other dogs safely and appropriately is essential for their well-being.

Introducing Your Maltese to Other Dogs

1. **Neutral Territory**: Start by introducing your Maltese to other dogs in a neutral setting, like a park or a friend's yard, to reduce territorial instincts.
2. **Use Leashes for Control**: Keep both dogs on a leash during the initial interaction, allowing them to sniff each other calmly. Hold the leash loosely to avoid creating tension.
3. **Observe Body Language**: Watch for signs of comfort or discomfort, such as tail wagging, relaxed posture, or signs of fear like cowering or growling.
4. **Limit the Interaction**: Keep the first few meetings brief and end on a positive note. Gradually increase interaction time as they become more comfortable.

Encouraging Positive Play

If your Maltese seems comfortable with another dog, you can encourage gentle play. However, remember that Maltese are small and fragile compared to larger breeds, so supervision is necessary.

1. **Redirect Rough Play**: If the other dog plays too roughly, step in and redirect their attention to prevent your Maltese from feeling overwhelmed.
2. **Reward Positive Behavior**: Praise and reward your Maltese with treats for calm, friendly interactions to reinforce good behavior.
3. **Teach Commands**: Commands like "come" and "stay" can be useful for controlling interactions and ensuring safety.

By following these guidelines, you can help your Maltese feel at ease around other dogs and avoid conflicts.

Safe Ways to Socialize with Other Pets

Other dogs, your Maltese may encounter other animals such as cats, rabbits, or small pets. Introducing them in a safe, controlled manner is essential to prevent fear, aggression, or unwanted chasing behavior.

Introducing Your Maltese to Cats

1. **Controlled Meeting**: Keep your Maltese on a leash during the first interaction, and ensure the cat has a safe escape route.
2. **Observe Reactions**: Watch how each pet responds, giving them time to adjust to each other's presence. If either shows signs of stress, separate them and try again later.
3. **Supervision and Patience**: Some dogs and cats form bonds quickly, while others need more time. Always supervise interactions until you're confident both are comfortable together.

Introducing Your Maltese to Small Pets

For households with small pets like birds, rabbits, or guinea pigs, introduce your Maltese with caution.

1. **Teach Boundaries**: Use commands like "stay" and "leave it" to prevent your Maltese from getting too close or overly curious.
2. **Controlled Environment**: Keep small pets in a secure cage or pen when introducing them, allowing your Maltese to sniff from a safe distance.
3. **Supervised Visits**: Even if they seem to get along, always supervise interactions to ensure safety.

With patience and positive reinforcement, your Maltese can learn to coexist peacefully with other household pets.

Socializing Adult Dogs

While socializing a puppy is ideal, it's never too late to work on socialization with an adult Maltese. However, it may take a bit more time and patience.

Building Positive Associations

1. **Gradual Exposure**: Start by introducing your Maltese to new experiences slowly, such as taking them to a quiet park or exposing them to new sounds at home.
2. **Reward-Based Training**: Reward your dog with treats, praise, or play whenever they respond positively to a new situation, building positive associations.
3. **Stay Calm**: Dogs pick up on their owner's emotions. By staying calm and positive, you help your Maltese feel more comfortable.

Desensitization Techniques

Desensitization helps your dog become accustomed to new situations gradually. For example, if your Maltese is fearful of other dogs, start by having them observe other dogs from a distance and slowly reduce the distance over time.

Professional Help

If your adult Maltese exhibits significant fear or aggression, consult a professional dog trainer or behaviorist who specializes in socialization. They can provide personalized strategies and ensure your Maltese learns safely and effectively.

Greeting New People

Introducing your Maltese to new people is an important part of socialization. Some Maltese may be naturally friendly, while others may be more reserved.

Positive First Impressions

1. **Calm Introductions**: Ask new people to approach your Maltese slowly, allowing the dog to initiate contact if they feel comfortable.
2. **Avoid Overwhelming**: Avoid crowding or too much excitement when introducing your dog to new people, as it can lead to anxiety.
3. **Use Treats**: Encourage new people to offer treats, helping your Maltese associate strangers with positive experiences.

Teaching Basic Commands

Teaching your Maltese commands like "sit," "stay," and "down" can be beneficial when meeting new people. These commands provide structure and help them feel secure.

1. **"Sit" Command**: Ask your Maltese to sit when new people arrive, creating a calm interaction.
2. **"Stay" Command**: The "stay" command can prevent your dog from jumping on guests or becoming overly excited.

Following these steps makes the greeting experience more enjoyable and comfortable for everyone involved.

Maltese and Children

Maltese dogs are generally friendly and patient, making them suitable companions for families with children. However, as a small breed, they are also more delicate and may feel overwhelmed by young or energetic children. Teaching both the dog and children how to interact respectfully is key.

Teaching Children to Respect Your Maltese

1. **Gentle Touch**: Teach children how to pet the Maltese gently, avoiding rough handling, tail pulling, or squeezing.
2. **Supervised Interactions**: Always supervise young children when they are around the Maltese to ensure everyone stays safe.
3. **Recognize Warning Signs**: Educate children about signs that a dog wants space, such as moving away, growling, or hiding. Encourage them to give the Maltese space if they exhibit these behaviors.

Establishing Boundaries

Small dogs like Maltese can become defensive if they feel threatened. Set boundaries to help keep interactions calm and enjoyable.

1. **Create Safe Zones**: Provide your Maltese with a quiet place, like a crate or bed, where they can retreat if they need a break from interaction.
2. **Limit Overexcitement**: Maltese may become anxious around high-energy children. Encourage calm behavior, especially when the dog is eating, resting, or playing with toys.
3. **Reward Positive Behavior**: Praise and reward your Maltese when they interact calmly and positively with children, reinforcing good behavior.

Introducing Maltese Puppies to Children

If you're introducing a Maltese puppy to children, early socialization is essential.

1. **Expose Gradually**: Start with short interactions, allowing the puppy and children to get comfortable with each other.
2. **Teach Commands Early**: Training your puppy to respond to commands like "sit" and "come" can make interactions smoother and help the puppy learn boundaries.
3. **Involve Children in Care**: Allowing children to participate in the puppy's care, such as feeding or brushing, helps build a positive bond between them.

By teaching children and your Maltese mutual respect and boundaries, you can foster a positive, safe relationship that will last a lifetime.

Socialization is a crucial aspect of raising a well-mannered, confident Maltese. By helping your Maltese navigate interactions with other dogs, pets, new people, and children, you're setting them up for a happier and more fulfilling life. With patience, positive reinforcement, and attention to their unique needs, your Maltese will become a cherished companion capable of thriving in various social situations.

CHAPTER 8

Maltese and Your Other Pets

The Maltese is known for its friendly and adaptable nature, which makes it a wonderful companion not only for families but also for households that already have other pets. However, introducing a new Maltese, whether it's a puppy or an older dog, into a household with existing pets can require careful planning and patience. In this chapter, we'll explore the process of interspecies introductions, introducing an older Maltese to other pets, addressing aggression or bad behavior, distinguishing between rough play and aggression, and the challenges and considerations of raising multiple puppies from the same litter.

Interspecies Introductions

Introducing a Maltese to other animals, whether it's a cat, rabbit, or even a larger dog, requires a gentle approach. Your Maltese may have no experience with other species, and it's important to ensure that the introduction is positive for both your Maltese and your other pets.

Preparing for the Introduction

1. **Neutral Territory**: If possible, introduce your pets in a neutral space. This could be a room neither of them has spent much time in. This reduces territorial instincts and helps both animals feel less defensive.

2. **Keep Them Separated Initially**: Before the actual face-to-face meeting, allow the animals to smell each other through a door or baby gate. This helps them become accustomed to each other's scent without direct interaction.

3. **Supervised Interaction**: Once both animals seem comfortable, begin the introduction under supervision. Keep your Maltese on a leash and allow the other pet to roam freely. Monitor body language from both animals. A calm demeanor, relaxed posture, and wagging tail are good signs, while growling, hissing, or tense posture indicate that one or both pets may need more time to adjust.

Introducing a Maltese to Cats

Maltese dogs typically do well with cats, but each pet has its own temperament. A proper introduction can help prevent stress and conflict.

1. **Let the Cat Lead**: Cats can be territorial, so it's important to let your cat approach at its own pace. Never force the two animals to interact. Allow your Maltese to observe the cat without direct contact at first.
2. **Positive Reinforcement**: Reward both your Maltese and your cat with treats and praise when they show calm behavior. This helps them associate each other with positive experiences.
3. **Slow and Steady**: Gradually increase the amount of time they spend together as long as they both remain calm. Over time, they may start to form a bond, or at the very least, tolerate each other peacefully.

Introducing a Maltese to Larger Dogs

If you have a larger dog, introducing a Maltese puppy or adult dog should be done with care, as size differences can lead to accidental injury during play.

1. **Control the Environment**: Keep your Maltese on a leash and make sure the larger dog is also under control. Watch for signs of rough play or

excitement in the larger dog that could overwhelm the smaller Maltese.

2. **Separate During Mealtimes**: To avoid any food-related aggression, it's best to feed both dogs in separate areas until you're sure they are comfortable sharing space.

3. **Monitor Play**: Larger dogs may accidentally hurt a small Maltese during rough play, so always supervise interactions. Encourage calm behavior and intervene if the play becomes too boisterous.

Introducing an Older Maltese

Introducing an older Maltese to a household with existing pets can be different from introducing a puppy. Adult dogs may have established habits and behaviors that could affect how they react to other pets. An older Maltese may also be set in its ways, making the adjustment period a little longer.

Steps for Introducing an Older Maltese

1. **Respect Boundaries**: An older Maltese may not have the same playful energy as a puppy, so it's important to introduce them slowly and respect their need for personal space. Allow your older Maltese to adjust to its new environment and pets at its own pace.

2. **Supervised Interactions**: Always supervise the first few meetings between an older Maltese and your existing pets. If the older dog shows signs of discomfort, such as growling or snapping, give them space and try again later. Consistent short introductions can help reduce tension over time.

3. **Separate Space**: Ensure your older Maltese has a designated space where they can retreat if they feel overwhelmed. A comfortable bed or crate in a quiet part of the house can provide a safe space where your dog can relax.

4. **Positive Reinforcement**: Just like with puppies, reward calm and friendly behavior with treats and praise. This helps reinforce the idea that getting along with other pets leads to positive outcomes.

Aggression/Bad Behavior

In some cases, introducing a Maltese to other pets may lead to aggression or bad behavior. This could be due to fear, territorial instincts, or a lack of socialization. It's important to address these issues early to prevent them from becoming long-term problems.

Recognizing Aggression

1. **Body Language**: Signs of aggression include growling, barking, raised fur, a stiff posture, and baring teeth. If your Maltese or other pets display any of these behaviors, it's important to separate them immediately to prevent escalation.
2. **Resource Guarding**: If your Maltese shows aggression around food, toys, or other resources, this is known as resource guarding. This behavior can be managed by feeding pets in separate areas and removing high-value toys during interactions.
3. **Fear-Based Aggression**: Some dogs become aggressive when they feel afraid or threatened. In these cases, it's important to create a safe environment where your Maltese feels secure.

Managing Bad Behavior

1. **Training**: Basic obedience training can help manage bad behavior. Commands like "sit," "stay," and "leave it" can be useful in situations where your Maltese might become aggressive.
2. **Consult a Professional**: If aggression or bad behavior persists, it may be necessary to consult a professional dog trainer or behaviorist. They can help you develop a plan to manage your Maltese's behavior and ensure peaceful coexistence with other pets.

Rough Play or Aggression?

Distinguishing between rough play and aggression can be tricky, especially when you have multiple pets. Maltese dogs, like other breeds, may engage in rough play that can sometimes look like aggression. However, it's important to recognize the difference to ensure the safety of all pets.

Recognizing Rough Play

1. **Play Bows**: Dogs often signal their intent to play with a play bow, where they lower their front legs while keeping their back end up. This is a clear sign that your Maltese is engaging in playful behavior.
2. **Happy Expressions**: During rough play, dogs may growl, bark, or nip, but their body language remains relaxed. A wagging tail, open mouth, and relaxed posture indicate playfulness rather than aggression.
3. **Take Breaks**: If your Maltese and other pets take breaks during rough play, this is a good sign. Playful dogs often stop to catch their breath or drink water before resuming play.

Signs of Aggression During Play

1. **Stiff Posture**: If your Maltese's body becomes stiff, or if the other pet is showing signs of discomfort, such as trying to get away or yelping, the play may be turning aggressive.
2. **Escalation**: If the intensity of the play continues to escalate without breaks, or if one pet seems overwhelmed, it's time to step in and separate them.
3. **Biting or Pinning**: Biting that causes injury or one dog pinning the other to the ground is a sign that the play has become too rough. Separate the pets and allow them to calm down before trying again.

Raising Multiple Puppies from the Same Litter

Raising multiple puppies from the same litter, also known as "littermates," can be rewarding but also challenging. While Maltese dogs are known for their affectionate nature, having two puppies at the same time requires extra effort and attention to prevent behavioral issues.

The Challenges of Raising Littermates

1. **Littermate Syndrome**: One of the main concerns when raising two puppies from the

same litter is the development of "littermate syndrome." This occurs when the puppies become overly bonded with each other, leading to issues like separation anxiety, aggression towards other dogs, or difficulty forming a bond with their human family.

2. **Individual Attention**: To prevent littermate syndrome, it's important to spend time with each puppy individually. This helps them develop confidence on their own and form a strong bond with you.

3. **Separate Training**: Train each puppy separately to ensure they learn obedience commands and develop independence. If you train them together, they may become distracted by each other, making it harder for them to focus on you.

Benefits of Raising Littermates

1. **Companionship**: Raising two puppies from the same litter can provide built-in companionship. They can play together, which helps burn off energy and reduces boredom.

2. **Easier Socialization**: Puppies raised together often learn social cues from each other, which can make the socialization process easier.

3. **Shared Experiences**: Littermates that are raised together often have a deep bond and can provide

emotional comfort to each other in stressful situations.

Best Practices for Raising Littermates

1. **Crate Them Separately**: While it may be tempting to allow your Maltese puppies to share a crate, it's best to crate them separately. This helps them become comfortable being alone and prevents over-reliance on each other.
2. **Separate Feeding**: Feed your puppies in separate areas to prevent competition or food guarding. This also helps them learn to eat calmly without distraction.
3. **Regular Vet Visits**: Ensure both puppies receive regular veterinary care, and monitor their growth and development. Some health issues may not be immediately apparent, so regular check-ups are essential.

Raising multiple Maltese dogs, whether puppies from the same litter or with other pets, requires a thoughtful approach. With proper training, supervision, and care, your Maltese can thrive alongside other pets, forming harmonious relationships within your household.

CHAPTER 9

Exercising Your Maltese — Physically and Mentally

Exercising your Maltese is essential to keep them healthy, happy, and well-behaved. While the Maltese is a small breed, they are lively, curious, and need both physical and mental stimulation to stay content. This chapter covers everything you need to know about exercising your Maltese, including their exercise requirements, ways to make exercise fun, and tips for keeping them mentally engaged. By understanding their needs, you can create an exercise routine that strengthens the bond between you and your dog while promoting their overall well-being.

Exercise Requirements

Maltese dogs have moderate exercise needs compared to larger, high-energy breeds, but they still require a daily routine to burn off energy and prevent boredom. A lack of exercise can lead to unwanted behaviors like chewing, barking, and digging as your dog finds ways to release their pent-up energy.

Daily Physical Exercise

1. **Short Walks**: A Maltese generally benefits from two short walks each day, totaling about 20-30 minutes. Due to their small size, they may not need long hikes or intense exercise. Walking gives them an opportunity to explore new scents, enjoy the outdoors, and practice socialization with other dogs or people they may encounter.

2. **Playtime**: Maltese dogs love play sessions, which can be done indoors or outdoors. A 15-20 minute play session can add variety to their exercise routine and provide mental stimulation. Games like fetch, tug-of-war, and hide-and-seek are especially engaging for Maltese dogs and help them release energy in a controlled, enjoyable way.

3. **Structured Exercise**: For a bit of added structure, you can try short agility courses or obedience training sessions. The Maltese is an intelligent breed that thrives on learning new skills and commands, making this an ideal way to challenge them both physically and mentally.

4. **Individual Needs**: While most Maltese dogs do well with the above guidelines, each dog is unique. Younger dogs or particularly active Maltese may require more exercise, while senior dogs may be content with shorter walks and gentle play. Always observe your dog's energy levels to adjust their routine as needed.

Age-Appropriate Exercise

1. **Puppies**: Young Maltese puppies should have short, gentle play sessions to prevent overstressing their developing bodies. Frequent, brief periods of play are ideal, and you should avoid intense exercise or long walks until they are older.
2. **Adults**: Adult Maltese typically have higher endurance and benefit from a consistent exercise routine. Aim to engage them with varied activities to keep their interest and provide them with adequate physical and mental outlets.
3. **Senior Dogs**: Older Maltese may have lower energy levels, but they still need regular, gentle exercise to keep their muscles strong and prevent weight gain. Short, slow-paced walks or light play sessions are usually sufficient for seniors, but be mindful of any physical limitations.

How to Make Exercise Fun

Exercise is more enjoyable when it doesn't feel like a chore for you or your Maltese. By making it fun, you'll both look forward to each session. Here are some creative ways to make exercise more engaging for your Maltese.

Interactive Games

1. **Fetch with a Twist**: Traditional fetch is a great exercise, but you can make it more stimulating by introducing different toys or playing in varied environments. A small, soft ball or lightweight toy is ideal for a Maltese, and you can play indoors if you have enough space. Adding in new toys now and then keeps your dog excited and mentally engaged.
2. **Tug-of-War**: Many Maltese enjoy tug-of-war, a game that combines physical exercise with bonding. Use a soft, durable rope toy to avoid injury, and make sure to let your dog win occasionally to boost their confidence.
3. **Hide-and-Seek**: This game involves hiding treats or a favorite toy around the house or yard, encouraging your Maltese to use their nose and curiosity to find them. It's an excellent way to provide mental stimulation and encourage

problem-solving. Start by making the hiding spots easy to find and gradually increase the difficulty as your dog becomes more experienced.

Incorporate Training into Exercise

1. **Obedience Drills**: Adding obedience drills into playtime can make exercise more mentally stimulating. Commands like "sit," "stay," and "come" can be practiced as part of a game. For example, play a version of "Simon Says" where your Maltese has to follow a command to continue the game.

2. **Agility Training**: While Maltese dogs are small, they are agile and quick. Setting up a simple agility course in your backyard or a nearby park can provide both physical and mental exercise. Try using items like small hurdles, tunnels, or weaving poles to challenge your dog's agility and coordination. Start with basic movements and reward your dog with treats or praise to encourage them.

3. **Trick Training**: Maltese dogs are eager learners and often enjoy learning new tricks. Teaching tricks like "spin," "high five," or "roll over" provides both mental stimulation and bonding time. Tricks can be incorporated into exercise

routines, keeping your Maltese entertained and reinforcing their training.

Changing Up Routine

1. **Explore New Locations**: Walking the same route daily can become monotonous for your Maltese. Try taking them to different parks, nature trails, or even pet-friendly stores to keep things fresh. The new environment, scents, and sights will make each outing an adventure.
2. **Incorporate Toys and Obstacles**: Add some variety to your play sessions by using different toys or incorporating obstacles. Use soft toys, small hurdles, or interactive puzzle toys to keep your Maltese engaged and excited about exercise.
3. **Group Playdates**: If your Maltese is friendly with other dogs, setting up playdates can be a great way to socialize and exercise at the same time. A playdate in a fenced yard or at a dog park offers them a chance to burn off energy while making new friends.

Tips for Keeping Your Dog Occupied

Keeping your Maltese mentally engaged is as important as physical exercise. Without proper mental stimulation, Maltese dogs can become bored and exhibit unwanted behaviors. Here are some ideas for keeping your dog's mind occupied and helping them stay entertained.

Interactive Toys

1. **Puzzle Toys**: Puzzle toys are excellent for providing mental stimulation and keeping your Maltese occupied for extended periods. Toys that require your dog to work for treats, such as treat-dispensing balls or puzzle boards, can provide both physical and mental exercise. Start with simpler toys and gradually increase the difficulty as your Maltese becomes more adept.

2. **Kong Toys**: Stuffing a Kong toy with peanut butter or treats can keep your Maltese busy for a while, especially if they enjoy chewing. Freezing the stuffed toy can make the challenge last even longer, providing mental stimulation as your dog works to extract the treats.

3. **Hide Treats Around the House**: This simple activity keeps your dog occupied and allows them to practice their natural sniffing instincts. Hide small treats or kibble in various locations and let your Maltese sniff them out. Start with easy hiding spots, and as they get better at the game, increase the difficulty.

Training as Mental Stimulation

1. **Teach New Commands**: Teaching your Maltese new commands or tricks provides mental exercise and helps reinforce your bond. Regular training sessions keep them mentally sharp and give them something to focus on. Tricks like "shake," "spin," and "crawl" are fun for Maltese dogs to learn and easy to practice indoors.

2. **Clicker Training**: Clicker training is a reward-based training method that can keep your Maltese engaged. Each time they perform the desired behavior, click and reward them with a treat. The clicker helps them understand exactly which action you're rewarding, making learning faster and more precise.

3. **Advanced Obedience**: If your Maltese has mastered basic commands, consider moving to more advanced obedience training. Commands like "fetch my slippers" or "find the toy" provide mental stimulation and challenge them to think through tasks.

DIY Indoor Activities

1. **Obstacle Course**: Create a simple indoor obstacle course using household items like chairs, cushions, and blankets. Guide your Maltese through the course and reward them with treats or praise. This activity provides physical

exercise and keeps them mentally engaged, especially on rainy days when outdoor exercise isn't possible.

2. **Shell Game**: Place a treat under one of three cups, shuffle the cups, and then let your Maltese choose the one with the treat. This game challenges their problem-solving abilities and can be repeated with increasing difficulty.

3. **Find the Toy**: Hide your dog's favorite toy somewhere in the house and encourage them to find it. Start with easy locations and gradually increase the difficulty. The "find it" command helps your Maltese use their sense of smell and provides mental stimulation.

Enrichment Activities

1. **Scent Work**: Maltese dogs, while not traditionally scent-driven, still enjoy using their noses to explore. You can use simple scent work activities to engage their natural curiosity. Hide treats around the house and encourage your Maltese to find them, or set up a scent trail for them to follow.

2. **Socialization Outings**: Taking your Maltese to pet-friendly events or locations provides both socialization and mental stimulation. New people, environments, and other dogs offer

enrichment that can help them adapt better to various situations.

3. **Rotate Toys**: Rather than leaving all toys available all the time, rotate a selection of toys every week. This keeps toys "new" and exciting for your Maltese, reducing boredom and increasing engagement with each toy when it reappears.

Managing Rest Periods

Just as important as exercise, rest is essential for your Maltese. After playtime or training, allow your dog to rest and recharge. This prevents over-exertion and ensures that each exercise session remains enjoyable. Resting also gives them time to mentally process new information, helping them retain what they've learned in training.

Incorporating both physical and mental exercise into your Maltese's daily routine can make a big difference in their behavior, health, and happiness. Regular exercise tailored to your Maltese's needs, combined with mental enrichment, creates a balanced, rewarding lifestyle for your dog. With consistent effort, you'll find that your Maltese is not only physically fit but also mentally satisfied and a delight to have around.

CHAPTER 10

Training Your Maltese

Training your Maltese is one of the most important aspects of pet ownership. Proper training not only fosters good behavior but also strengthens the bond between you and your dog. Maltese are intelligent, eager to please, and highly trainable, making them excellent candidates for various types of training. This chapter covers the benefits of training, effective methods, and tips for successful training at home. By investing time in training your Maltese, you will enjoy a well-mannered pet that is a joy to be around.

Benefits of Proper Training

Training your Maltese provides numerous benefits that enhance your relationship with your dog and contribute to their overall happiness and well-being.

Improved Behavior

One of the most significant advantages of training is improved behavior. A well-trained Maltese is less likely to engage in unwanted behaviors such as excessive barking, chewing, or jumping on people. Training establishes boundaries and teaches your dog what is expected of them, making life more enjoyable for both of you.

Enhanced Communication

Training creates a two-way communication channel between you and your Maltese. Through commands and cues, you can convey your expectations, while your dog learns to understand and respond to your requests. This communication fosters a deeper bond and mutual respect.

Socialization Skills

Training often involves socializing your Maltese with other dogs, people, and various environments. Properly socialized dogs are more confident and less fearful, which can reduce anxiety and aggression. Socialization also helps your Maltese develop good manners in different situations, making outings more pleasant.

Mental Stimulation

Training is not just about learning commands; it also provides mental stimulation. Engaging your Maltese in training exercises helps keep their mind sharp and prevents boredom, which can lead to behavioral issues. Mental challenges, such as obedience training and puzzle-solving, can be very fulfilling for your dog.

Safety and Control

A well-trained Maltese is easier to manage in various situations, enhancing their safety and yours. Commands like "sit," "stay," and "come" can be lifesavers in potentially dangerous scenarios, such as when your dog encounters an aggressive animal or approaches a busy street.

Training Your Maltese at Home

Training your Maltese can be a rewarding experience that you can do in the comfort of your own home. With patience, consistency, and a positive attitude, you can teach your dog essential commands and good behavior.

Creating a Training Schedule

Establishing a consistent training schedule is crucial for success. Short, frequent training sessions (5-10 minutes) are often more effective than longer sessions. Aim for multiple sessions throughout the day, especially when your Maltese is alert and engaged.

Setting Up a Training Area

Choose a quiet space in your home where distractions are minimal. This area should be free from noise and other pets to help your Maltese focus on learning. Keep training supplies, such as treats, toys, and clickers, readily available in this space.

Incorporating Training into Daily Life

Training does not have to be limited to scheduled sessions. You can incorporate training into daily activities. For example, practice commands before feeding your Maltese, during walks, or while playing. This approach helps reinforce training and makes learning feel natural.

Using the Right Equipment

Having the proper equipment can enhance your training experience. A comfortable harness or collar, a leash, and high-value treats can make training more enjoyable for your Maltese. Consider using a clicker as a training tool to mark desired behaviors, making it easier for your dog to understand what you want.

Maintaining Clear Expectations

Establishing and maintaining clear expectations is key to successful training. Consistency and clarity in commands and rewards help your Maltese understand what you want from them.

Consistency in Commands

Use the same words and tone for commands consistently. For example, if you choose to use "sit," do not switch to "sit down" or "sit now." Consistency helps your Maltese learn faster and reduces confusion.

Consistent Rewards

Always reward desired behaviors immediately after your Maltese performs the action. This can be in the form of treats, praise, or playtime. Consistent rewards reinforce good behavior and motivate your Maltese to repeat the action.

Establishing Boundaries

Clearly defined boundaries help your Maltese understand their limits. Be firm but fair, and ensure everyone in your household follows the same rules. This consistency reinforces the expectations you set for your dog.

Handling Mistakes

Mistakes are part of the training process. If your Maltese doesn't understand a command or makes an error, stay calm and patient. Instead of scolding, redirect their behavior and try again. This approach encourages learning without creating fear or anxiety.

Basic Commands

Teaching basic commands is the foundation of effective training. These commands not only promote good behavior but also enhance communication between you and your Maltese.

Sit

1. **How to Teach**: Hold a treat close to your Maltese's nose, then move your hand upwards, allowing their head to follow the treat. This motion will cause their bottom to lower. Once they are in the sitting position, say "sit" and reward them with the treat.
2. **Practice**: Repeat the process several times until your Maltese understands the command. Gradually reduce the use of treats, replacing them with praise.

Stay

1. **How to Teach**: First, have your Maltese sit. Open your palm in front of you and say "stay." Take a few steps back. If your Maltese stays in place, return to them, praise, and reward. If they move, gently guide them back and try again.
2. **Practice**: Gradually increase the distance and duration of the "stay" command over time. This command is essential for keeping your Maltese safe in various situations.

Come

1. **How to Teach**: Start with your Maltese on a leash. Say "come" while gently pulling on the leash. When your dog approaches you, reward them with praise and treats.
2. **Practice**: Once they consistently respond to the command on a leash, practice it in a safe, enclosed area without the leash, gradually increasing the distance.

Down

1. **How to Teach**: With your Maltese in a sitting position, hold a treat in your hand close to the ground. Lower the treat while saying "down." As your dog lowers their body to reach the treat, reward them.

2. **Practice**: Repeat this command, gradually phasing out the treat and rewarding them only with praise.

Leave It

1. **How to Teach**: Place a treat in your hand and show it to your Maltese. Close your fist around the treat and say "leave it." Once they stop trying to get the treat, reward them with a different treat.
2. **Practice**: Gradually increase the difficulty by placing treats on the ground while using the "leave it" command.

Other Useful Commands

The basic commands, you may also consider teaching your Maltese other useful commands, such as "heel," "wait," and "no." These commands can help keep your Maltese safe and well-behaved in various situations.

Methods of Training

There are several training methods you can employ to teach your Maltese effectively. Choosing the right method depends on your dog's personality and learning style.

Alpha Dog Training

The alpha dog training method is based on establishing dominance over your dog. While some dog owners have used this approach in the past, modern training techniques focus more on cooperation than dominance. Many trainers now believe that using harsh techniques or asserting dominance can create fear and lead to behavioral issues.

Positive Reinforcement

Positive reinforcement is a highly effective training method that encourages desired behaviors through rewards. This approach focuses on reinforcing good behavior with treats, praise, or playtime. Positive reinforcement strengthens the bond between you and your Maltese and helps them learn faster.

1. **Benefits**: This method promotes a trusting relationship and reduces anxiety, making it a popular choice for training small breeds like the Maltese.
2. **Implementation**: When your Maltese exhibits the desired behavior, immediately reward them. For example, if they come to you when called, give them a treat and praise them enthusiastically.

Clicker Training

Clicker training is a form of positive reinforcement that uses a clicker to mark desired behaviors. The click sound acts as a signal that your Maltese has done something right, followed by a reward.

1. **Benefits**: The clicker helps your Maltese associate the sound with positive outcomes, making it an effective training tool.
2. **Implementation**: Begin by clicking the device when your Maltese performs the desired behavior, then follow up with a treat. Over time, your Maltese will associate the click with good behavior.

Lure and Reward

The lure and reward method involves using treats to guide your Maltese into the desired position or behavior. This method is especially effective for commands like "sit" and "down."

1. **Benefits**: This method provides a clear visual cue for your Maltese, making it easier for them to understand what is expected.
2. **Implementation**: Use treats to lure your Maltese into the desired position and reward them immediately when they comply.

Dangers of Negative Reinforcement

While training your Maltese, it's crucial to understand the potential dangers of negative reinforcement. Negative reinforcement involves punishing undesirable behaviors, which can lead to fear and anxiety in your dog.

Creating Fear and Anxiety

Using harsh methods, such as yelling or physical punishment, can create fear in your Maltese. A fearful dog may become anxious, aggressive, or withdraw from interaction, making it more difficult to train them.

Damaging the Bond

Negative reinforcement can damage the bond between you and your Maltese. When training feels like a punishment, your dog may begin to associate you with negative experiences. This bond is essential for effective training, as a trusting relationship encourages cooperation and responsiveness.

Ineffectiveness

Research has shown that positive reinforcement is more effective than negative reinforcement in training. Dogs trained with positive methods are more likely to repeat desired behaviors and develop a strong bond with their owners.

When to Hire a Trainer

While many pet owners successfully train their dogs at home, there are times when hiring a professional trainer is beneficial. A professional can provide valuable guidance, especially for first-time dog owners or those facing specific challenges.

Recognizing the Need for Professional Help

1. **Behavioral Issues**: If your Maltese exhibits severe behavioral issues, such as aggression or extreme anxiety, a professional trainer can provide strategies to address these concerns.
2. **Lack of Progress**: If you feel stuck or frustrated with your Maltese's training, a trainer can offer fresh perspectives and new techniques to help your dog learn.
3. **Socialization**: If your Maltese struggles with socialization, a trainer can guide you through proper introductions and socialization techniques.

Choosing the Right Trainer

When looking for a trainer, consider their qualifications, experience, and training methods. Seek out trainers who use positive reinforcement techniques, as these methods are more effective and beneficial for your dog.

1. **Ask for Recommendations**: Talk to other pet owners or your veterinarian for recommendations. Online reviews and local training schools can also provide valuable insights.
2. **Attend Classes**: Many trainers offer group classes or private sessions. Attending a class can give you a feel for the trainer's style and effectiveness.
3. **Set Goals**: Clearly communicate your training goals to the trainer. This collaboration helps ensure that you and your Maltese receive the most appropriate training for your needs.

Training your Maltese is an ongoing journey that requires time, patience, and consistency. By understanding the benefits of training, utilizing effective methods, and maintaining clear expectations, you can foster a well-behaved and happy companion. Whether you choose to train at home or enlist the help of a professional, the effort you put into training will strengthen your bond and enhance your Maltese's quality of life. A well-trained Maltese is not only a joy to live with but also a source of pride for any dog owners.

CHAPTER 11

Traveling with Your Maltese

Traveling with your Maltese can be an exciting adventure. Whether you are flying to a new destination or going on a road trip, taking your furry companion along can enhance your experience. However, traveling with a small breed like the Maltese requires careful planning to ensure their comfort and safety. This chapter covers everything you need to know about traveling with your Maltese, including flying, hotel stays, kenneling, and tips for a smooth journey.

Flying with Your Dog

Flying with your Maltese can be a convenient way to reach your destination. However, it's essential to prepare adequately to ensure a stress-free experience for both you and your pet.

Choosing the Right Airline

Not all airlines have the same policies regarding traveling with pets. Before booking your flight, research airlines that are known for their pet-friendly policies. Look for airlines that allow small dogs in the cabin, as this is usually the most comfortable option for your Maltese. Check their pet travel guidelines, including weight limits, carrier specifications, and fees associated with flying your dog.

Preparing for the Flight

Preparation is key to a successful flight with your Maltese. Here are some important steps to take before heading to the airport:

1. **Get Your Dog Used to the Carrier**: Choose an airline-approved carrier that is well-ventilated and large enough for your Maltese to stand, turn around, and lie down comfortably. Introduce your Maltese to the carrier well in advance of your flight, allowing them to explore it and spend time inside. Use treats and praise to create positive associations with the carrier.

2. **Visit the Veterinarian**: Schedule a visit to your veterinarian to ensure your Maltese is healthy enough for travel. Obtain a health certificate, which some airlines require, stating that your dog is fit for flying. Discuss any concerns you may have about traveling with your Maltese, especially if they have pre-existing health conditions.

3. **Pack Essentials**: Pack a travel bag for your Maltese that includes food, water, collapsible bowls, a leash, waste bags, and any medications they may need. Also, consider bringing a favorite toy or blanket to provide comfort during the journey.
4. **Plan for Meals**: Feed your Maltese a light meal a few hours before the flight to minimize the chances of motion sickness. Avoid feeding them immediately before the flight, as this can lead to discomfort during travel.

At the Airport

Arrive at the airport early to allow plenty of time for check-in and security procedures. Here are some tips for navigating the airport with your Maltese:

1. **Check-In**: When checking in, inform the airline staff that you are traveling with a pet. Follow their instructions regarding paperwork and fees. Keep your Maltese calm and comfortable while waiting for your flight.
2. **Security Screening**: At security, you may be required to remove your Maltese from the carrier and carry them through the metal detector while the carrier goes through the X-ray machine. Make sure your Maltese is leashed and secure during this process to prevent any escape.

3. **Waiting Areas**: While waiting for your flight, find a quiet area where you and your Maltese can relax. Take them for a short walk to stretch their legs before boarding.

During the Flight

Once you're on the plane, follow these guidelines to ensure a smooth experience for your Maltese:

1. **Keep Them Calm**: If your Maltese is anxious during the flight, try to soothe them with gentle petting and reassuring words. You can also offer treats to create a positive experience.
2. **Limit Movement**: Keep your Maltese in their carrier during the flight. Opening the carrier can lead to a stressful situation if they escape. Make sure the carrier is securely fastened under the seat in front of you.
3. **Hydration**: Offer water to your Maltese during the flight, especially on longer journeys. A collapsible bowl works well for this purpose. You can also use a wet washcloth to hydrate them if they are reluctant to drink.
4. **Monitor for Signs of Stress**: Pay attention to your Maltese's behavior throughout the flight. Signs of stress can include excessive barking, whining, or attempts to escape the carrier. If your

dog seems uncomfortable, speak softly to them and offer calming treats if necessary.

Hotel Stays with Your Dog

Finding a pet-friendly hotel is essential for a smooth travel experience. Not all accommodations allow dogs, so it's important to do your research in advance.

Finding Pet-Friendly Hotels

When planning your trip, search for hotels that welcome pets. Websites like BringFido or Expedia allow you to filter results based on pet policies. Here are some tips for finding the right hotel:

1. **Read Reviews**: Look for reviews from other pet owners who have stayed at the hotel. They can provide valuable insights into the hotel's pet policy, accommodations, and staff attitude toward pets.
2. **Call Ahead**: Even if a hotel advertises as pet-friendly, it's a good idea to call ahead to confirm their specific policies regarding pets. Ask about any breed or size restrictions, additional fees, and pet amenities.
3. **Check for Amenities**: Some hotels offer pet-friendly amenities, such as dog beds, treats, and designated walking areas. Look for hotels

that provide these extra touches to enhance your stay.

Preparing for Your Stay

Once you've booked your hotel, prepare for your stay with these tips:

1. **Pack Your Dog's Essentials**: Just as with flying, pack your Maltese's essentials for the hotel stay. This includes food, water bowls, a leash, waste bags, and any favorite toys or blankets to help them feel at home.
2. **Familiarize Your Dog with the Room**: When you arrive at the hotel, allow your Maltese to explore the room. Set up a comfortable space for them with their bed and toys, and take a few moments to reassure them in their new surroundings.
3. **Establish Routines**: Maintain your Maltese's regular routines as much as possible, including feeding, bathroom breaks, and exercise. Consistency will help reduce anxiety and make your dog feel more secure.

Hotel Etiquette

While staying at a hotel with your Maltese, be mindful of the following etiquette tips:

1. **Keep Noise Levels Down**: Be respectful of other guests by keeping noise levels to a minimum. If your Maltese tends to bark, consider bringing along some calming treats or toys to keep them occupied.
2. **Use Designated Areas for Potty Breaks**: Always take your Maltese to designated potty areas and clean up after them promptly. Carry waste bags with you at all times to ensure you're prepared for any situation.
3. **Never Leave Your Dog Alone**: Most hotels discourage leaving pets unattended in the room. If you need to leave your Maltese for any reason, consider using doggie daycare services or asking hotel staff if they can recommend a local pet sitter.

Kenneling vs. Dog Sitters

If you're planning a longer trip and cannot take your Maltese along, you may need to consider alternative care options. The two main choices are kenneling and hiring a dog sitter. Each option has its advantages and disadvantages.

Kenneling Your Maltese

Kenneling can be a suitable option for some pet owners, but it's essential to choose the right facility.

1. **Pros**: Kennels often provide structured care and socialization opportunities for dogs. They typically have trained staff who can monitor your Maltese's well-being and handle any emergencies.
2. **Cons**: Some dogs may experience anxiety or stress in a kennel environment, especially if they are not used to being away from their owners. It's crucial to find a kennel that provides a safe and comfortable atmosphere for your Maltese.

Hiring a Dog Sitter

Hiring a dog sitter can be a more personalized option for your Maltese. Here are some points to consider:

1. **Pros**: A dog sitter can provide one-on-one attention in your home or theirs, allowing your Maltese to stay in a familiar environment. This option can reduce stress and anxiety, as your dog will not have to adapt to a new setting.
2. **Cons**: It's essential to find a reliable and trustworthy sitter. Conduct thorough research, including checking references and reading reviews, to ensure your Maltese will be in good hands.

Making the Right Choice

Ultimately, the choice between kenneling and hiring a dog sitter depends on your Maltese's personality, your travel plans, and your comfort level. If your dog is sociable and enjoys interacting with other dogs, a kennel may be a great fit. However, if your Maltese is more anxious or has specific needs, a dog sitter may be the better option.

Choosing the Right Boarding Facility

If you decide to kennel your Maltese, selecting the right boarding facility is crucial. Follow these steps to ensure you make the best choice:

Research Facilities

Start by researching local boarding facilities. Look for reviews online and ask for recommendations from friends or your veterinarian. Create a list of potential facilities to visit.

Schedule Tours

Once you have a list of facilities, schedule tours to visit them in person. Pay attention to the following:

1. **Cleanliness**: The facility should be clean, well-maintained, and free of unpleasant odors. A clean environment is essential for your dog's health and well-being.
2. **Safety**: Ensure the boarding area is secure and has appropriate fencing. Check for hazards, such as sharp objects or toxic plants, that could pose risks to your Maltese.
3. **Staff Interaction**: Observe how staff members interact with the dogs. They should be friendly, knowledgeable, and attentive to the animals in their care.

Ask Questions

During your visit, ask questions to gauge the facility's suitability for your Maltese:

1. **Staff-to-Dog Ratio**: Inquire about the number of staff members compared to the number of dogs in the facility. A lower staff-to-dog ratio ensures more individualized attention for your Maltese.
2. **Daily Activities**: Ask about the daily routine for dogs in the facility. Ensure that your Maltese will have opportunities for exercise, playtime, and socialization.
3. **Emergency Procedures**: Find out what protocols the facility has in place for emergencies, including veterinary care. It's important to know

that your Maltese will receive prompt attention if needed.

Trust Your Instincts

Ultimately, trust your instincts when choosing a boarding facility. If something feels off during your visit, or if you don't feel confident in the staff's abilities, continue your search until you find a place where you feel comfortable leaving your Maltese.

Special Tips and Tricks for Traveling

To make your travel experience with your Maltese even smoother, consider the following tips and tricks:

Create a Travel Checklist

Before you embark on your journey, create a travel checklist to ensure you have everything you need for your Maltese. Include items like food, water, bowls, leash, waste bags, grooming supplies, medications, and any favorite toys or blankets.

Keep Identification Up to Date

Ensure your Maltese has proper identification, including a collar with an ID tag and a microchip. This is crucial in case your dog gets lost during your travels.

Plan for Breaks

If you're driving to your destination, plan for regular breaks during the trip. Stop every couple of hours to allow your Maltese to stretch their legs, drink water, and relieve themselves. This will help prevent restlessness and discomfort.

Consider Your Dog's Comfort

During the journey, prioritize your Maltese's comfort. Use a pet seatbelt or a secure crate in the car to keep them safe. Maintain a comfortable temperature in the vehicle, and avoid leaving them alone in the car for extended periods.

Prepare for Emergencies

Familiarize yourself with emergency veterinary clinics at your travel destination. Keep a list of important contacts, including your veterinarian's phone number and any local pet services, in case you need assistance.

Stay Calm

Dogs often pick up on their owner's emotions. If you remain calm and relaxed, your Maltese is more likely to feel the same way. Practice deep breathing and positive affirmations to keep stress levels low during travel.

Traveling with your Maltese can be a rewarding experience that strengthens your bond and creates lasting memories. By preparing in advance, choosing the right accommodations, and ensuring your dog's comfort and safety, you can make every trip enjoyable for both you and your furry friend. Whether flying, staying in hotels, or finding care while you're away, the key is to plan ahead and consider your Maltese's needs every step of the way. With the right preparation and mindset, you can embark on new adventures with your beloved Maltese, creating cherished memories together.

CHAPTER 12

Grooming Your Maltese

Grooming your Maltese is not just about maintaining their beautiful coat; it's also essential for their overall health and well-being. Regular grooming helps to keep their skin clean, reduces the risk of health issues, and strengthens the bond between you and your furry friend. This chapter will cover the essential aspects of grooming your Maltese, including coat basics, grooming tools, bathing and brushing techniques, nail trimming, ear and eye cleaning, dental care, and when to seek professional help.

Coat Basics

The Maltese breed is known for its long, silky white coat that is both beautiful and unique. However, this coat requires regular care to keep it looking its best. Understanding the basics of the Maltese coat is essential for effective grooming.

Coat Structure

Maltese dogs have a double coat made up of a soft undercoat and long, straight outta hair. Unlike many other breeds, Maltese do not shed much, which can be beneficial for allergy sufferers. However, the lack of shedding means that their hair can mat easily if not groomed regularly. Regular brushing helps to remove loose hairs, dirt, and debris, preventing tangles and matting.

Hair Growth Patterns

Maltese hair grows continuously, meaning they do not have a seasonal shedding period. Instead, their hair can grow up to 8 to 10 inches long if not trimmed. Many Maltese owners opt for a shorter "puppy cut" for easier maintenance. This cut keeps the hair short and manageable while still showcasing the breed's distinct appearance.

Skin Health

Healthy skin is vital for a Maltese's overall well-being. Regular grooming allows you to check for any signs of skin issues, such as redness, irritation, or lumps. It's also an excellent opportunity to examine your Maltese for parasites like fleas and ticks. Ensuring that your Maltese has a healthy diet rich in essential fatty acids can also contribute to a healthy coat and skin.

Basic Grooming Tools

Having the right grooming tools is essential for effective grooming. Investing in high-quality equipment will make the grooming process easier and more enjoyable for both you and your Maltese. Here are some basic grooming tools you should have:

Brushes and Combs

1. **Slicker Brush**: This brush is great for removing tangles and mats. Its fine, bent wires penetrate deep into the coat, lifting out loose hair and debris.
2. **Pin Brush**: Ideal for smoothing out the coat and giving it a polished finish. The pin brush can also help remove any remaining tangles after using a slicker brush.
3. **Wide-Toothed Comb**: A wide-toothed comb is perfect for detangling the hair and getting rid of knots, especially around the ears and under the legs.

Grooming Scissors

Invest in a good pair of grooming scissors for trimming the hair around your Maltese's face, paws, and bottom. Blunt-tipped scissors are recommended for safety, especially around sensitive areas. Some owners also find it helpful to have thinning shears to reduce bulk and create a more natural look.

Nail Clippers

A good pair of dog nail clippers or a nail grinder is essential for keeping your Maltese's nails at a healthy length. Regular nail trimming helps to prevent painful splitting and breaking, which can lead to injury.

Ear Cleaning Supplies

Having a gentle ear cleaner and cotton balls or pads is crucial for maintaining ear health. Regularly cleaning your Maltese's ears can help prevent infections and other issues.

Toothbrush and Dog Toothpaste

Dental care is a vital aspect of grooming. A soft-bristled toothbrush and dog-specific toothpaste will help keep your Maltese's teeth healthy and clean.

Bathing and Brushing

Bathing and brushing your Maltese are two of the most critical grooming tasks. Regular baths keep their coat clean and healthy, while brushing prevents mats and tangles.

Bathing Your Maltese

1. **Frequency**: Maltese dogs should be bathed every 3 to 4 weeks, depending on their activity level and lifestyle. If they spend a lot of time outdoors, they may need more frequent baths.
2. **Choosing the Right Shampoo**: Use a mild, dog-specific shampoo that is gentle on the skin and coat. Avoid human shampoos, as they can strip the natural oils from your Maltese's skin, leading to dryness and irritation.
3. **Bathing Process**:
   - Begin by brushing your Maltese to remove any tangles or mats before the bath.
   - Use lukewarm water to wet their coat thoroughly, avoiding the head initially.
   - Apply a small amount of shampoo and lather it gently into the coat, being careful to avoid their eyes and ears.
   - Rinse thoroughly until all shampoo is removed, as residue can irritate the skin.

- After rinsing, consider applying a dog conditioner for added moisture and softness.
- Gently dry your Maltese with a towel, and if they are comfortable with it, you can use a blow dryer on a low setting.

Brushing Your Maltese

1. **Daily Routine**: Daily brushing is recommended to prevent tangles and mats. Focus on the areas that are more prone to matting, such as behind the ears, under the legs, and around the collar.
2. **Technique**: Start by using a slicker brush to remove tangles, working from the ends of the hair toward the roots. Follow up with a pin brush to smooth out the coat and give it a polished appearance.
3. **Checking for Skin Issues**: While brushing, take the time to check your Maltese's skin for any signs of irritation, lumps, or parasites. Early detection of issues can lead to more effective treatment.

Nail Trimming

Nail trimming is a crucial part of grooming that many pet owners overlook. Overgrown nails can lead to pain, discomfort, and even joint issues.

How to Trim Nails

1. **Frequency**: Trim your Maltese's nails every 3 to 4 weeks. Regular trimming helps to prevent the nails from becoming too long.
2. **Tools**: Use a pair of dog nail clippers or a nail grinder. Some owners prefer using grinders because they can be less stressful for the dog and provide a smoother finish.
3. **Trimming Process**:
   - Choose a quiet, well-lit area where your Maltese feels comfortable.
   - Hold their paw gently but firmly. Press the pad slightly to extend the nail for easier trimming.
   - Identify the quick, which is the pink part of the nail that contains blood vessels. Avoid cutting this area, as it can be painful and bleed.
   - Trim only the tip of the nail, gradually shortening it to avoid cutting too much at once.

- Reward your Maltese with treats and praise after trimming to create a positive association with the process.

Cleaning the Ears and Eyes

Maintaining the health of your Maltese's ears and eyes is essential for their overall well-being. Regular cleaning helps to prevent infections and other issues.

Ear Cleaning

1. **Frequency**: Clean your Maltese's ears every 2 to 4 weeks, or more often if they are prone to ear infections.
2. **Supplies Needed**: Use a dog-specific ear cleaner and cotton balls or pads.
3. **Cleaning Process**:
   - Gently lift the ear flap and apply a small amount of ear cleaner into the ear canal.
   - Massage the base of the ear for about 20 seconds to help loosen debris.
   - Let your Maltese shake their head, then use a cotton ball to wipe away any dirt and wax from the ear flap and canal.
   - Avoid using cotton swabs, as they can push debris further into the ear.

Eye Cleaning

Maltese dogs are prone to tear staining, which can affect their appearance and comfort.

1. **Frequency**: Clean your Maltese's eyes as needed, typically every few days, depending on their tear production.
2. **Supplies Needed**: Use a soft, damp cloth or specialized eye wipes for dogs.
3. **Cleaning Process**:
    ○ Gently wipe away any discharge from the corner of the eyes, using a separate part of the cloth for each eye.
    ○ For tear stains, consider using a specially formulated tear stain remover to help reduce staining over time.

Dental Care

Dental health is often overlooked, but it is an essential aspect of grooming that can significantly impact your Maltese's overall health.

Importance of Dental Care

Poor dental hygiene can lead to dental disease, which can cause pain, tooth loss, and infections. Additionally, bacteria from the mouth can enter the bloodstream, leading to serious health issues in other organs, such as the heart.

How to Care for Your Maltese's Teeth

1. **Frequency**: Aim to brush your Maltese's teeth at least 2 to 3 times a week. Daily brushing is ideal for optimal dental health.
2. **Tools Needed**: Use a soft-bristled toothbrush and dog-specific toothpaste. Never use human toothpaste, as it can be harmful to dogs.
3. **Brushing Process**:
   - Start by letting your Maltese taste the toothpaste to get them used to the flavor.
   - Lift their lip and gently brush the outer surfaces of their teeth, focusing on the back teeth where plaque tends to build up.
   - Gradually work your way to the front teeth, ensuring you're gentle and not causing discomfort.

Additional Dental Care Options

Consider incorporating dental chews or toys into your Maltese's routine to help reduce plaque buildup. Regular veterinary dental cleanings may also be necessary, depending on your Maltese's individual dental health.

When to Seek Professional Help

While regular grooming at home is crucial, there are times when professional help may be necessary.

Grooming Services

If you're uncomfortable grooming your Maltese yourself, consider seeking help from a professional groomer. They can provide services like haircuts, baths, and nail trims, ensuring your Maltese looks and feels their best.

Veterinary Care

Regular check-ups with your veterinarian are vital for monitoring your Maltese's health. If you notice any unusual behavior, changes in appetite, or signs of discomfort, schedule a visit as soon as possible. Your veterinarian can also provide guidance on grooming best practices and address any specific health concerns related to grooming.

Grooming your Maltese is a vital part of their care that contributes to their health and happiness. By understanding their coat basics, using the right tools, and following effective grooming practices, you can keep your Maltese looking beautiful while ensuring their well-being. Regular grooming also provides an opportunity for bonding and allows you to monitor your dog's health closely. Whether you choose to groom at home or seek professional help, a consistent grooming routine will help your Maltese thrive.

CHAPTER 13

Basic Health Care

Ensuring that your Maltese receives proper health care is crucial for a long and happy life. This chapter covers the fundamentals of health care for your Maltese, including vet visits, parasite prevention, vaccinations, common health conditions, holistic options, and pet insurance. With regular care and awareness, you can keep your Maltese healthy and happy for many years.

Visiting the Vet

Regular vet visits are essential to monitor your Maltese's health and catch any potential health issues early.

How Often to Visit the Vet

1. **Puppies**: Young Maltese puppies require frequent vet visits to monitor growth, administer vaccinations, and check for any early health issues. Expect to visit the vet every 3-4 weeks during the first few months of life.

2. **Adults**: Healthy adult Maltese dogs should visit the vet annually for a wellness check. During these visits, the vet will conduct a physical examination, update vaccinations, and run any necessary tests.
3. **Seniors**: As your Maltese ages (usually around seven years), they may require more frequent vet visits—typically every six months. Aging dogs are more prone to health issues, so regular exams allow for early detection and treatment.

What to Expect During a Vet Visit

During a typical vet visit, your Maltese will undergo a full physical exam. This includes checking their eyes, ears, mouth, skin, coat, and general body condition. Your vet may also recommend blood work, especially as your Maltese ages, to check for underlying health issues.

Building a Relationship with Your Vet

Developing a strong relationship with your vet is essential. A vet who understands your dog's health history is better equipped to detect subtle changes that could indicate health problems. Don't hesitate to ask questions and discuss any concerns you have about your Maltese's health or behavior.

Fleas and Ticks

Parasites like fleas and ticks can cause significant discomfort and health problems for your Maltese, so prevention is key.

Recognizing Fleas and Ticks

1. **Fleas**: Fleas are tiny, dark brown insects that live on your dog's skin and feed on their blood. Signs of fleas include itching, redness, and small black specks (flea dirt) in your dog's fur.
2. **Ticks**: Ticks are larger than fleas and attach themselves to your dog's skin to feed. They often hide in crevices, like around the ears or between toes. You may notice a small lump where a tick has attached.

Preventing Fleas and Ticks

1. **Topical Treatments**: These treatments, applied directly to your dog's skin, provide protection against fleas and ticks for about a month.
2. **Oral Medications**: Oral flea and tick preventatives are often effective for a month and work by entering your dog's bloodstream.
3. **Tick Checks**: After spending time outdoors, especially in wooded or grassy areas, check your

Maltese for ticks. Prompt removal reduces the risk of diseases like Lyme disease.

Removing Ticks

If you find a tick on your Maltese, use a pair of tweezers to grasp it as close to the skin as possible and pull it out gently but firmly. Avoid twisting, as this can leave parts of the tick embedded in the skin. Clean the area with antiseptic afterward.

Intestinal Worms and Parasites

Intestinal parasites can affect your Maltese's health, causing symptoms like weight loss, diarrhea, and a dull coat.

Types of Intestinal Parasites

1. **Roundworms**: Common in puppies, roundworms can cause bloating and digestive issues.
2. **Hookworms**: These parasites attach to the intestinal lining, leading to blood loss and anemia.
3. **Tapeworms**: Tapeworms are usually spread by fleas. You may notice small white segments around your dog's anus.

Symptoms of Parasite Infection

Symptoms of intestinal parasites include weight loss, poor coat condition, vomiting, diarrhea, and a pot-bellied appearance. Some infections can be asymptomatic, so regular deworming is recommended.

Preventing and Treating Intestinal Parasites

1. **Regular Deworming**: Most vets recommend deworming puppies every few weeks and continuing with regular treatment as adults.
2. **Sanitary Practices**: Keep your Maltese's living environment clean, and dispose of feces promptly to reduce the risk of reinfection.
3. **Preventing Fleas**: Since some parasites, like tapeworms, are spread by fleas, controlling fleas also helps prevent parasite infections.

Vaccinations

Vaccinations are essential for protecting your Maltese against common and potentially deadly diseases.

Core Vaccinations

1. **Distemper**: Distemper is a highly contagious and often fatal disease affecting the respiratory and nervous systems.
2. **Parvovirus**: Parvovirus is a severe gastrointestinal infection, particularly dangerous for puppies.
3. **Adenovirus**: This virus can cause hepatitis, impacting the liver and potentially leading to death.
4. **Rabies**: Rabies is a fatal disease that can be transmitted to humans. Most areas require dogs to be vaccinated against rabies by law.

Non-Core Vaccinations

Depending on your Maltese's lifestyle and region, your vet may recommend additional vaccines:

1. **Bordetella**: This vaccine protects against kennel cough, which is highly contagious in places like dog parks or boarding facilities.
2. **Lyme Disease**: If you live in an area with a high tick population, your vet may recommend a Lyme disease vaccine.
3. **Leptospirosis**: Spread through water contaminated by wildlife, leptospirosis can cause kidney and liver damage.

Common Diseases and Conditions

While Maltese dogs are generally healthy, they are prone to certain health conditions.

Patellar Luxation

Patellar luxation is a common issue in small breeds where the kneecap dislocates from its normal position, causing lameness and discomfort. Surgery may be necessary for severe cases.

Dental Disease

Due to their small mouths, Maltese dogs are prone to dental issues. Regular brushing and professional cleanings are essential to prevent periodontal disease.

White Shaker Syndrome

This neurological disorder causes tremors in small white dogs, including Maltese. Medication can help control the tremors.

Allergies

Maltese can suffer from allergies, which may manifest as itching, skin irritation, or digestive issues. Identifying and avoiding triggers, along with veterinary treatment, can help manage symptoms.

Holistic Alternatives and Supplements

Holistic care can complement traditional veterinary care, promoting overall wellness in your Maltese.

Omega-3 Fatty Acids

Omega-3 fatty acids, often found in fish oil supplements, are beneficial for your dog's coat and skin. They also have anti-inflammatory properties that can help with arthritis and joint pain.

Probiotics

Probiotics support digestive health by maintaining a healthy balance of bacteria in the gut. They can be helpful for dogs with digestive issues or those recovering from illness.

Glucosamine and Chondroitin

These supplements are beneficial for joint health, especially in older dogs. They support cartilage health and reduce symptoms of arthritis.

Herbs

Herbs can offer natural health benefits, but always consult your vet before introducing herbs to your Maltese's diet.

Milk Thistle

Milk thistle is known for its liver-supporting properties. It can be especially beneficial for dogs on medications that may affect the liver.

Chamomile

Chamomile has calming properties and can help with anxiety and digestive upset. It's available in tea or supplement form, but be cautious with dosage.

Turmeric

Turmeric has anti-inflammatory properties and is often used to support joint health and manage pain. However, turmeric can interact with certain medications, so consult your vet.

CBD Oil

CBD oil has gained popularity for its potential health benefits for dogs, including Maltese. Derived from the hemp plant, CBD oil is non-psychoactive and may help with a variety of issues.

Potential Benefits of CBD Oil

1. **Pain Relief**: CBD oil may help manage pain from arthritis, injuries, or other conditions.
2. **Anxiety Reduction**: Some owners find that CBD oil helps calm anxious dogs, especially during stressful events like fireworks.
3. **Anti-Inflammatory Properties**: CBD has anti-inflammatory effects that may benefit dogs with joint or skin conditions.

How to Use CBD Oil

1. **Dosage**: Always start with a low dose and gradually increase, monitoring your dog for any adverse reactions.
2. **Quality Matters**: Use high-quality, veterinary-recommended CBD oil, as not all products on the market are safe or effective.
3. **Consult Your Vet**: Speak with your vet before giving your Maltese CBD oil, especially if they are on other medications.

Pet Insurance

Pet insurance can help cover the cost of unexpected veterinary bills, providing peace of mind.

Why Consider Pet Insurance

1. **Unexpected Expenses**: Accidents and illnesses can lead to costly vet bills. Pet insurance can alleviate the financial burden.
2. **Chronic Conditions**: Some pet insurance plans cover chronic conditions, making ongoing treatments more affordable.
3. **Preventative Care**: Some policies include wellness coverage, which can help cover routine care costs like vaccinations and check-ups.

Choosing a Pet Insurance Plan

When selecting pet insurance, consider factors such as coverage limits, reimbursement rates, and waiting periods. Some plans cover only accidents, while others offer comprehensive coverage for illnesses and preventive care. Be sure to read the policy carefully to understand what is covered and any exclusions.

Basic health care is essential to your Maltese's well-being. By keeping up with regular vet visits, preventing parasites, staying on top of vaccinations, and understanding common health conditions, you can ensure your Maltese leads a healthy life. Holistic supplements, herbs, and CBD oil can offer additional support, while pet insurance provides financial security in case of unexpected health expenses. Together, these efforts will contribute to a long, healthy, and happy life for your Maltese companion.

CHAPTER 14

Nutrition for Your Maltese

Proper nutrition is essential for maintaining your Maltese's health and well-being. Understanding the various aspects of dog food, including the benefits of quality options, different types of commercial foods, and how to prepare homemade meals, will help ensure your furry friend gets the best possible diet. This chapter will explore these topics in depth, providing valuable insights into feeding your Maltese.

Benefits of Quality Dog Food

Choosing quality dog food can have numerous benefits for your Maltese. Here are some key advantages:

1. Improved Overall Health

Quality dog food is formulated with balanced nutrients that support your Maltese's overall health. These nutrients include essential proteins, carbohydrates, fats, vitamins, and minerals, all of which contribute to optimal bodily functions.

- **Healthy Coat**: A diet rich in omega fatty acids helps maintain a shiny, healthy coat, reducing shedding and skin issues.
- **Strong Immune System**: A balanced diet supports a strong immune system, helping your Maltese fight off infections and diseases.
- **Optimal Weight**: High-quality foods are formulated to provide the right amount of calories for your dog's size, helping maintain a healthy weight.

2. Better Digestion

Premium dog foods often contain high-quality ingredients that are easier to digest. This means less gas, bloating, and upset stomachs.

- **Fiber**: Good dog food includes the right amount of fiber to promote healthy digestion and prevent constipation.
- **Probiotics**: Some brands add probiotics, which support gut health and improve nutrient absorption.

3. Increased Energy Levels

A balanced diet provides your Maltese with the energy needed for daily activities. Quality dog food ensures they get the right fuel for their playful and energetic nature, making them more active and alert.

4. Enhanced Longevity

Quality nutrition plays a significant role in your dog's lifespan. Dogs fed high-quality food are generally healthier and may live longer, healthier lives compared to those on a poor diet.

5. Reduced Health Problems

Feeding your Maltese high-quality food can help prevent many common health problems, such as obesity, diabetes, and dental issues. Quality dog food is designed to meet the specific nutritional needs of your dog's breed and size, reducing the likelihood of health issues associated with poor nutrition.

Types of Commercial Dog Foods

When selecting dog food for your Maltese, you'll encounter several types of commercial foods. Understanding these options will help you make an informed decision.

1. Dry Dog Food (Kibble)

Dry dog food, also known as kibble, is one of the most popular choices for dog owners. It is convenient, affordable, and has a long shelf life.

- **Pros**:
    - ○ Economical and easy to store.
    - ○ Helps keep teeth clean due to the crunchy texture.
    - ○ Available in various formulas tailored to specific needs (e.g., age, size, and health conditions).
- **Cons**:
    - ○ Some lower-quality kibble may contain fillers and artificial additives.
    - ○ Less moisture, which may be a concern for dogs that require more hydration.

2. Wet Dog Food (Canned)

Wet dog food, packaged in cans or pouches, has a higher moisture content, which can be beneficial for hydration.

- **Pros**:
    - ○ Palatable and often more appealing to picky eaters.
    - ○ Higher moisture content can help dogs that don't drink enough water.
- **Cons**:

o More expensive than dry food and has a shorter shelf life once opened.

o May contribute to dental issues due to lack of crunch.

3. Semi-Moist Dog Food

Semi-moist dog food comes in packets and has a chewy texture.

- **Pros**:
  o Convenient and often very palatable for dogs.
  o Easy to serve and store.
- **Cons**:
  o Often contains more sugar and artificial preservatives compared to other types.
  o Less commonly used than dry or wet food.

4. Raw Diets

Some dog owners opt for raw diets, consisting of uncooked meat, bones, fruits, and vegetables.

- **Pros**:
  o Can lead to shinier coats and healthier skin.

- High protein content supports muscle development.
- **Cons**:
  - Requires careful preparation to ensure a balanced diet and prevent contamination.
  - Not suitable for all dogs and may require veterinary guidance.

5. Freeze-Dried and Dehydrated Foods

These foods are minimally processed and retain most of their nutrients.

- **Pros**:
  - Lightweight and easy to store.
  - Retain the nutrients of raw food while being shelf-stable.
- **Cons**:
  - More expensive than traditional dog food.
  - Requires rehydration before feeding.

Ingredients to Watch Out For

Not all dog foods are created equal. When selecting a dog food for your Maltese, be mindful of certain ingredients that could be harmful or of low quality.

1. Fillers

Fillers like corn, soy, and wheat are often used to bulk up dog food but provide little nutritional value.

- **Why to Avoid**: These ingredients can lead to allergies and digestive issues in some dogs and may contribute to weight gain.

2. Artificial Additives

Look for foods free of artificial colors, flavors, and preservatives.

- **Why to Avoid**: These additives serve no nutritional purpose and may negatively impact your Maltese's health over time.

3. By-Products

By-products can include various animal parts that are not typically considered food for human consumption.

- **Why to Avoid**: The quality and source of by-products can be questionable, and they often contain low-quality protein.

4. Excessive Fillers

Dog foods with high amounts of starches and sugars can lead to obesity and other health problems.

- **Why to Avoid**: Maltese are prone to dental issues, and sugary foods can exacerbate these problems.

5. Low-Quality Proteins

Avoid foods that list vague terms like "meat meal" or "animal by-products."

- **Why to Avoid**: Look for specific protein sources, such as chicken, beef, or fish, to ensure your Maltese is getting quality protein.

Categories of Dog Food

Understanding the different categories of dog food can help you choose the best option for your Maltese.

1. Complete and Balanced

Foods labeled as "complete and balanced" meet the nutritional standards established by the Association of American Feed Control Officials (AAFCO). This means they contain all the necessary nutrients in the right proportions for your dog.

2. Premium Dog Food

Premium dog foods often contain higher-quality ingredients and fewer fillers. They tend to be more expensive but provide better nutrition.

3. Limited Ingredient Diets

These diets are formulated with fewer ingredients, making them ideal for dogs with food sensitivities or allergies. They focus on a single protein source and limited carbohydrates.

4. Grain-Free Diets

Grain-free foods have become popular in recent years, with many dog owners opting for these options to avoid potential allergies. However, recent studies suggest a possible link between grain-free diets and canine dilated cardiomyopathy (DCM), so consult your vet before making this switch.

Homemade Dog Food

Some pet owners choose to prepare homemade meals for their Maltese. This option can provide control over ingredients and quality, but it requires careful planning to ensure balanced nutrition.

1. Benefits of Homemade Dog Food

- **Control Over Ingredients**: You can select high-quality ingredients, avoiding fillers and artificial additives.
- **Customization**: Tailor meals to your dog's specific dietary needs, preferences, and allergies.

2. Nutritional Balance

To create a balanced homemade diet, consult with a veterinarian or canine nutritionist. Key components of a homemade dog diet include:

- **Proteins**: Lean meats like chicken, turkey, beef, or fish.
- **Carbohydrates**: Whole grains such as brown rice or quinoa, or vegetables like sweet potatoes.
- **Fats**: Healthy fats from sources like fish oil or flaxseed oil.
- **Vitamins and Minerals**: Include a variety of vegetables to provide essential vitamins and minerals.

3. Meal Preparation Tips

- **Cooking**: Cook meats thoroughly and avoid using any seasoning, as certain ingredients (like onions and garlic) can be toxic to dogs.
- **Storage**: Store homemade meals in airtight containers and freeze portions for future use.

Table Food: What Is Good, What Is Not?

Feeding your Maltese table food can be tempting, but not all human food is safe for dogs.

1. Safe Foods

Some human foods can be safe and healthy for your Maltese in moderation, such as:

- **Cooked Meat**: Chicken, turkey, and lean cuts of beef (without seasoning).
- **Vegetables**: Carrots, green beans, and sweet potatoes can be nutritious snacks.
- **Fruits**: Apples (without seeds), blueberries, and bananas can be healthy treats.

2. Foods to Avoid

Several foods can be harmful or toxic to dogs, including:

- **Chocolate**: Highly toxic and can cause serious health issues.
- **Grapes and Raisins**: Can lead to kidney failure in dogs.
- **Onions and Garlic**: Can damage red blood cells and cause anemia.
- **Alcohol**: Even small amounts can be deadly to dogs.

3. Moderation is Key

If you choose to share table food with your Maltese, do so in moderation. Overfeeding can lead to obesity, which is particularly concerning for small breeds like the Maltese.

Weight Management

Maintaining a healthy weight is crucial for your Maltese's overall health. Obesity can lead to various health issues, including diabetes, joint problems, and heart disease.

1. Monitoring Weight

Regularly weigh your Maltese and keep track of their weight. If you notice a significant gain, consult your veterinarian for advice on managing their diet.

2. Portion Control

Be mindful of portion sizes when feeding your Maltese. Follow feeding guidelines on the dog food packaging and adjust based on their activity level and weight.

3. Regular Exercise

Incorporate regular exercise into your Maltese's routine. Daily walks, playtime, and mental stimulation will help keep your dog fit and healthy.

4. Threat Management

Limit treats and high-calorie snacks. Instead, opt for healthier options like small pieces of fruits or vegetables.

5. Veterinary Guidance

Consult your veterinarian if you have concerns about your Maltese's weight. They can provide tailored advice and suggest specific diets or feeding plans.

Understanding nutrition is essential for your Maltese's health and longevity. By choosing quality dog food, being aware of harmful ingredients, considering homemade options, and monitoring their weight, you can help ensure your furry friend lives a healthy and happy life.

CHAPTER 15

Dealing with Unwanted Behaviors

Every dog owner will encounter unwanted behaviors at some point in their dog's life. Understanding these behaviors, identifying their root causes, and correcting them effectively are essential skills for any Maltese owner. This chapter will provide insights into what constitutes bad behavior, how to find the root of the problem, effective correction methods, and when to seek professional help.

What is Considered Bad Behavior?

Understanding what constitutes bad behavior in dogs is crucial for effective training. While each dog is unique, some common unwanted behaviors can frustrate owners and negatively impact the dog's quality of life.

1. Barking Excessively

While barking is a natural behavior for dogs, excessive barking can become a problem. This behavior may stem from excitement, boredom, anxiety, or a desire for attention.

- **Signs of Excessive Barking**: Continuous barking without a clear reason, barking at every noise or movement, and barking while alone.
- **Impact**: Excessive barking can lead to complaints from neighbors and can stress both the dog and owner.

2. Chewing and Destructive Behavior

Puppies and younger dogs are known for chewing, but adult dogs can also engage in this behavior. Destructive chewing can lead to ruined furniture, shoes, and other household items.

- **Signs of Chewing**: Finding chewed items, damaged furniture, or items missing from their usual places.
- **Impact**: Destructive chewing can create safety hazards and damage property.

3. Jumping Up

Jumping up on people is often viewed as an excited greeting behavior. However, it can become problematic when it leads to injuries or discomfort for guests and family members.

- **Signs of Jumping**: The dog jumps on people, especially when they enter the home or during playtime.
- **Impact**: Jumping can be embarrassing and lead to injuries, especially for elderly individuals or small children.

4. Aggression

Aggressive behavior can manifest in various ways, including growling, barking, or lunging. Aggression can occur due to fear, territorial instincts, or poor socialization.

- **Signs of Aggression**: Growling, snapping, or biting, as well as a stiff body posture and raised hackles.
- **Impact**: Aggression can lead to serious injuries and requires immediate attention.

5. Resource Guarding

Resource guarding occurs when a dog becomes protective of food, toys, or other possessions. This behavior can lead to aggression or conflicts with other pets or people.

- **Signs of Resource Guarding**: Growling, snapping, or stiffening when someone approaches their food or toys.
- **Impact**: Resource guarding can create tension within the household and can be dangerous.

6. Potty Training Issues

Housebreaking a dog can sometimes be challenging. Accidents in the house can lead to frustration for owners and can disrupt the home environment.

- **Signs of Potty Training Issues**: Frequent accidents indoors, despite established routines, or reluctance to go outside.
- **Impact**: Ongoing potty training issues can lead to stress for both the dog and owner.

7. Fear-Based Behaviors

Fear can lead to various unwanted behaviors, including hiding, barking, or destructive actions. Fear-based behaviors often arise from past experiences, lack of socialization, or environmental factors.

- **Signs of Fear-Based Behaviors**: Cowering, trembling, hiding, or avoidance of certain situations or people.

- **Impact**: Fear can significantly affect a dog's quality of life, limiting their experiences and interactions.

Finding the Root of the Problem

Understanding the underlying cause of unwanted behaviors is essential for effective training and correction. Here are steps to help identify the root of the problem:

1. Observe Your Dog

Spend time observing your Maltese in different situations. Take note of when the unwanted behavior occurs and the context surrounding it.

- **Environmental Factors**: Consider factors such as location, time of day, and the presence of other pets or people.
- **Triggers**: Identify potential triggers for the behavior, such as loud noises, unfamiliar people, or other animals.

2. Consider the Dog's History

Understanding your dog's past experiences can provide insight into their behavior.

- **Adoption Background**: If your Maltese is a rescue, consider their past environment and any traumatic experiences they may have faced.
- **Previous Training**: Assess any prior training methods that may have contributed to the behavior.

3. Evaluate Your Dog's Lifestyle

A dog's lifestyle significantly impacts their behavior.

- **Exercise Needs**: Maltese require regular physical activity and mental stimulation. Lack of exercise can lead to boredom and destructive behavior.
- **Socialization**: Evaluate your dog's socialization experiences. Insufficient exposure to different environments and people can contribute to fear and aggression.

4. Rule Out Medical Issues

Sometimes, unwanted behaviors stem from underlying medical issues. If your Maltese exhibits sudden changes in behavior, a visit to the veterinarian is necessary.

- **Health Check**: Schedule a veterinary check-up to rule out any medical conditions that may be causing discomfort or pain.

- **Behavioral Changes**: Sudden aggression, anxiety, or lethargy can indicate underlying health problems that require attention.

5. Seek Input from Family Members

If multiple people in your household interact with the dog, gather input from everyone.

- **Consistent Observations**: Discuss when and how the unwanted behavior occurs, ensuring everyone understands the context.
- **Common Responses**: Identify if anyone's responses to the behavior may inadvertently reinforce it.

How to Properly Correct Your Dog

Once you've identified the root cause of your Maltese's unwanted behavior, it's time to implement effective correction strategies. Here are some key approaches:

1. Positive Reinforcement

Positive reinforcement is one of the most effective training methods. Rewarding desired behaviors encourages your dog to repeat them.

- **Treats and Praise**: Use treats, verbal praise, or petting to reward good behavior immediately after it occurs.
- **Consistency**: Be consistent with rewards to reinforce the desired behavior over time.

2. Redirecting Behavior

Redirecting your dog to a more appropriate behavior can be an effective way to correct unwanted actions.

- **Distraction**: If your dog starts barking excessively, redirect their attention with a toy or engage them in a different activity.
- **Alternative Behaviors**: Teach your Maltese an alternative behavior to replace the unwanted one. For instance, if they jump, train them to sit instead.

3. Setting Boundaries

Establish clear boundaries to prevent unwanted behaviors. This can include setting up designated areas for your dog or using barriers to manage their environment.

- **Designated Areas**: Use baby gates or crates to restrict access to certain areas of the home.

- **Consistent Rules**: Ensure all family members enforce the same rules to provide consistency.

4. Training Sessions

Regular training sessions can help reinforce desired behaviors and discourage unwanted ones.

- **Short, Frequent Sessions**: Keep training sessions short and engaging to maintain your dog's interest.
- **Variety**: Include a variety of commands and tricks to keep things fun and stimulating.

5. Calm Leadership

As the owner, it's essential to exhibit calm and assertive leadership. Dogs often look to their owners for guidance, so maintaining a calm demeanor can help them feel secure.

- **Confident Energy**: Approach your dog with confidence to set the tone for your interactions.
- **Calm Corrections**: When correcting unwanted behavior, do so calmly without yelling or showing frustration.

6. Time-Outs

In certain situations, time-outs can be effective for correcting unwanted behaviors, particularly those involving aggression or hyperactivity.

- **Quiet Space**: Designate a quiet space for time-outs where your dog can calm down.
- **Duration**: Keep time-outs short (a few minutes) to prevent confusion.

7. Training Classes

Consider enrolling your Maltese in training classes to learn proper behavior and socialization skills in a controlled environment.

- **Group Classes**: These classes provide opportunities for socialization and learning from experienced trainers.
- **Professional Guidance**: Working with a professional trainer can provide valuable insights and personalized advice for your dog's needs.

When to Call a Professional

While many unwanted behaviors can be managed with the right training techniques, there are instances where professional help is necessary.

1. Severe Aggression

If your Maltese displays severe aggressive behavior, such as biting or lunging, seek professional help immediately. Aggression can pose a serious risk to people and other animals, and a qualified behaviorist can assess the situation and develop a safe training plan.

2. Persistent Anxiety

If your dog suffers from severe anxiety that affects their quality of life, consulting a professional can help. Anxiety can manifest in various ways, including destructive behavior, excessive barking, or withdrawal.

- **Behavioral Modification**: A professional can help develop a behavior modification plan tailored to your dog's needs.
- **Medication Options**: In some cases, medication may be necessary to help manage anxiety alongside behavior training.

3. Multiple Problem Behaviors

If your Maltese exhibits multiple unwanted behaviors, it may be beneficial to consult a professional. A behaviorist can identify patterns and provide a comprehensive plan to address each issue.

4. Lack of Progress

If you've tried various training methods without success, it may be time to seek help. Sometimes, a fresh perspective from a professional can make a significant difference in your dog's behavior.

5. Specific Behavioral Issues

Certain behavioral issues, such as separation anxiety, phobias, or obsessive-compulsive behaviors, may require specialized training. Professionals with experience in these areas can provide the necessary guidance and support.

6. Training for Advanced Skills

If you wish to train your Maltese for advanced skills, such as therapy work or agility, working with a professional trainer is beneficial. They can help you achieve your goals while ensuring your dog's safety and well-being.

By understanding what constitutes bad behavior, finding the root cause, and employing effective correction methods, you can help your Maltese become a well-mannered and happy companion. When in doubt, don't hesitate to seek the guidance of a professional to ensure your dog receives the best possible care and training.

CHAPTER 16

Caring for Your Senior Maltese

As Maltese dogs age, their needs change significantly. Senior Maltese require more attention, specific care, and sensitivity to ensure they live their later years comfortably and happily. In this chapter, we'll cover common ailments in senior Maltese, the essentials of basic senior dog care, illness and injury prevention, recommended supplements and nutrition, and how to recognize when it's time to say goodbye. We'll also address the sensitive and difficult topic of the euthanasia process.

Common Old-Age Ailments

Senior Maltese often experience health challenges similar to those of older humans. Recognizing the signs of common old-age ailments can help you provide the best care.

1. Arthritis

Arthritis is a common condition in older dogs, causing joint pain, stiffness, and limited mobility.

- **Signs**: Difficulty getting up, limping, reluctance to climb stairs, stiffness, and decreased interest in walks.
- **Care**: Regular, gentle exercise, weight management, and possibly medications recommended by a vet.

2. Cognitive Dysfunction Syndrome (CDS)

CDS, similar to dementia in humans, affects a dog's cognitive functions as they age.

- **Signs**: Confusion, disorientation, restlessness, pacing, and changes in sleep patterns.
- **Care**: Mental stimulation through gentle play, maintaining a routine, and sometimes medication prescribed by a vet.

3. Vision and Hearing Loss

As they age, many Maltese experience diminished eyesight and hearing.

- **Signs**: Bumping into furniture, increased vocalization, or lack of response to commands.

- **Care**: Avoid rearranging furniture, use hand signals, and avoid startling them.

4. Heart Disease

Older Maltese are at risk of developing heart disease, which can significantly affect their quality of life.

- **Signs**: Coughing, reduced tolerance for exercise, and labored breathing.
- **Care**: Monitoring by a vet, possibly with medication and dietary changes.

5. Dental Disease

Dental issues are common in senior dogs and can lead to other health problems if untreated.

- **Signs**: Bad breath, difficulty chewing, excessive drooling, and swollen gums.
- **Care**: Regular dental cleanings, soft food if needed, and daily brushing at home.

6. Kidney Disease

Senior Maltese are at risk for kidney disease, which can lead to serious health complications.

- **Signs**: Increased thirst, frequent urination, decreased appetite, and lethargy.

- **Care**: Special diets and regular vet visits for monitoring kidney function.

Understanding these ailments can help you recognize symptoms early and work with your veterinarian to manage your dog's condition effectively.

Basic Senior Dog Care

Caring for a senior Maltese requires adjustments to accommodate their changing needs. Here are key areas to focus on for your older companion's comfort and well-being.

1. Comfort and Accessibility

Ensure that your senior Maltese has a comfortable and accessible living space.

- **Soft Bedding**: Older dogs appreciate orthopedic beds that support their joints.
- **Reduced Mobility Challenges**: Provide ramps or stairs to help them access furniture or climb stairs.
- **Temperature Control**: Senior dogs are more sensitive to temperature extremes, so keep their environment comfortable.

2. Exercise and Mental Stimulation

Exercise remains important for senior dogs, but intensity and duration should be adjusted.

- **Gentle Walks**: Short, slow walks help maintain mobility without overexerting them.
- **Mental Stimulation**: Puzzle toys, light training sessions, and gentle play help keep their mind active.
- **Routine**: Stick to a regular schedule to provide structure and reduce stress.

3. Grooming and Hygiene

Regular grooming is essential to maintain the health of a senior Maltese's coat and skin.

- **Regular Brushing**: Prevents matting and keeps their coat soft, especially if they're less active and prone to tangles.
- **Nail Trimming**: Keep nails trimmed to prevent discomfort from overgrown nails that could affect mobility.
- **Frequent Bathing**: Use gentle, hypoallergenic shampoos suitable for their possibly sensitive skin.

4. Regular Vet Visits

Older dogs need more frequent vet check-ups to monitor for age-related health issues.

- **Twice-Yearly Exams**: Increased vet visits help catch early signs of illnesses common in older dogs.
- **Blood Tests and Diagnostics**: Regular blood work, X-rays, and other diagnostics can help monitor internal health, such as kidney or liver function.

Routine care and attention to these areas can greatly improve your senior Maltese's comfort and overall well-being.

Illness and Injury Prevention

Preventing illness and injury in a senior Maltese is essential to ensuring a healthy and happy life during their golden years.

1. Weight Management

Keeping a healthy weight minimizes stress on joints, which is crucial for avoiding arthritis and other mobility-related issues.

- **Portion Control**: Adjust portion sizes to match their reduced activity level.

- **Avoiding Treat Overuse**: Stick to healthy, low-calorie treats to prevent unnecessary weight gain.

2. Maintaining Clean Spaces

A clean living environment helps prevent infections, especially if your senior Maltese has a weakened immune system.

- **Frequent Cleaning**: Regularly clean bedding, toys, and living areas.
- **Disinfection**: Use pet-safe disinfectants to keep their environment as hygienic as possible.

3. Avoiding Risky Activities

Limit activities that pose an injury risk for your senior Maltese.

- **Monitor Playtime**: Keep activities low-impact and avoid excessive running or jumping.
- **Reduce Slippery Surfaces**: Place mats or rugs on slippery floors to prevent falls.

Preventing common illnesses and injuries helps improve the quality of life for a senior Maltese and keeps them healthier longer.

Supplements and Nutrition

Proper nutrition is critical for senior Maltese, and supplements can be beneficial for age-related issues.

1. High-Quality Protein

Older dogs require quality protein sources to support muscle maintenance without stressing the kidneys.

- **Lean Meats**: Chicken, turkey, and fish are excellent sources of protein for seniors.
- **Portion Control**: Adjust portions to match their reduced energy needs.

2. Joint Supplements

Supplements like glucosamine and chondroitin can alleviate arthritis symptoms and support joint health.

- **Glucosamine and Chondroitin**: These can reduce joint pain and improve mobility.
- **Omega-3 Fatty Acids**: Fish oil provides anti-inflammatory benefits that ease joint pain.

3. Antioxidants

Antioxidants help reduce cellular damage and may improve cognitive function in older dogs.

- **Vitamins C and E**: These can be found in food or as standalone supplements.
- **Blueberries**: A natural source of antioxidants that can be added as a treat.

4. Probiotics and Digestive Enzymes

As dogs age, their digestive efficiency may decline, so adding probiotics and enzymes can aid digestion.

- **Probiotics**: Help maintain gut health and prevent digestive upset.
- **Digestive Enzymes**: Improve nutrient absorption, supporting overall health.

Consult with your vet to determine the best diet and supplements for your senior Maltese.

When It's Time to Say Goodbye

Making the decision to say goodbye to a beloved pet is one of the most challenging aspects of pet ownership. Understanding when it's time is crucial to prevent prolonged suffering.

1. Signs of Decline

Recognizing signs of a declining quality of life can help guide your decision.

- **Pain and Discomfort**: If medication can't control pain, your dog may be suffering.
- **Loss of Interest**: When your dog no longer enjoys activities they once loved, it's a sign of declining quality of life.
- **Severe Illness**: Chronic or progressive illnesses that no longer respond to treatment are an indicator.

2. Assessing Quality of Life

Several quality-of-life scales can help assess your senior dog's well-being. These often consider factors like appetite, mobility, and happiness.

- **Mobility**: If they struggle to move, even with assistance, it may be time to consider their comfort.
- **Hygiene**: Loss of bladder or bowel control can impact dignity and comfort.
- **Appetite**: A sudden refusal to eat is often a signal of a more serious issue.

Discussing these factors with your vet can provide support and guidance in making the right choice.

How Will You Know When the Time Is Right?

The right time to say goodbye is a deeply personal decision, but there are some guiding factors.

1. Consulting with Your Vet

Veterinarians can offer objective perspectives and explain the medical realities of your dog's condition.

- **Medical Perspective**: A vet can explain whether treatments can provide relief or if the condition will worsen.
- **Support**: Veterinarians can provide emotional support and guidance through this difficult time.

2. Emotional Preparedness

Saying goodbye is emotionally painful, but knowing that you are ending suffering can bring peace.

- **Family Discussions**: Talk with family members about the decision to ensure everyone is prepared.
- **Honoring Memories**: Consider how to honor your Maltese's life, whether through keepsakes or other memorials.

3. Trusting Your Intuition

You know your dog better than anyone. Trusting your gut feeling can often provide the answer when facing this difficult decision.

The Euthanasia Process

Euthanasia is a humane option for ending a pet's suffering. Understanding the process can help prepare you for the experience.

1. Preparing for Euthanasia

Take time to create a calm, comforting environment for your dog.

- **Location**: Many vets offer the option to perform the procedure at home.
- **Familiar Surroundings**: Bring items like their favorite blanket or toy to help comfort them.

2. The Procedure

Your vet will explain each step, ensuring your Maltese experiences no pain or distress.

- **Sedation**: Most vets administer a sedative first, allowing your dog to relax.
- **Final Injection**: The euthanasia injection is painless, and your dog will drift off peacefully.

3. Aftercare and Grieving

After euthanasia, you may choose between burial, cremation, or other options for your pet's remains. Take time to grieve and honor your Maltese's memory in whatever way feels right for you.

Providing the right care for your senior Maltese helps them age gracefully and with dignity. With the right attention to health, comfort, and nutrition, you can make their golden years as joyful as possible. And when the time comes, knowing you've done everything possible for them will bring a sense of peace and closure.